COUNTED
CROSS-STITCH
PATCHWORK DESIGN

PEG FARRELL

PHOTOGRAPHY AND GRAPHICS
HOWARD SALTEN

VNR VAN NOSTRAND REINHOLD COMPANY
NEW YORK CINCINNATI TORONTO LONDON MELBOURNE

Dedication

To my mother for teaching me the love of a needle.

To Big H. for giving me time, space, and support.

Copyright © 1980 by Peg Farrell
Library of Congress Catalog Card Number 79-22980
ISBN 0-442-22375-7

Printed in the United States of America
Designed by Loudan Enterprises

Published by Van Nostrand Reinhold Company Inc.
135 West 50th Street, New York, NY 10020, U.S.A.

Van Nostrand Reinhold Australia Pty. Ltd.
480 Latrobe Street
Melbourne, Victoria 3000, Australia

Van Nostrand Reinhold Company Limited
Molly Millars Lane
Wokingham, Berkshire RG11 2PY, England

Macmillan of Canada
Division of Gage Publishing Limited
164 Commander Boulevard
Agincourt, Ontario M1S 3C7, Canada

16 15 14 13 12 11 10 9 8 7 6 5

Library of Congress Cataloging in Publication Data

Farrell, Peg.
    Counted Cross-Stitch Patchwork Design

    Bibliography: p.
    Includes index.
    1. Cross-stitch—Patterns. 2. Patchwork—Patterns.
I. Title.
TT778.C76F37   746.4′6   79-22980
ISBN 0-442-22375-7

Fabrics used for the designs in this book were provided courtesy of:
    Joan Toggitt Ltd.
    246 Fifth Ave.
    New York City, N. Y. 10001

    Art Needlework Treasure Trove
    Box 2440 Grand Central Station
    New York City, N. Y. 10017

The embroidery floss was provided courtesy of:
    The D.M.C. Corp.
    108 Trumbull St.
    Elizabeth, N. J. 07206

Shown on front jacket: Autumn Leaves, Christmas Star, Eight-Pointed Star, Le Moyne Star, Union Square, and Tree of Life.

Shown on back jacket: Cactus Rose, Blazing Star, Weather Vane, Joseph's Coat of Many Colors, Mosaic Variation, and Dolly Madison's Star.

CONTENTS

INTRODUCTION

This book is about combinations. It is primarily and most obviously a contemporary synthesis of two of the oldest, most practiced American needlecraft arts, patchwork and counted cross-stitch, but it is also an endless piecing together of design possibilities.

Some needlecraft publications have combined patchwork design and needlework with very beautiful solid color shapes and, of course, a variety of stitches for texture. To my eye, however, counted cross-stitch is by far the best medium for simulating the fabrics used in traditional quilts—the calico patterns, the prints, the plaids, and all the flower designs.

In this book I have collected some of the most well known and some of the least known quilt designs and adapted them to counted cross-stitch. This is not meant to be a quilt book, but rather a book that will teach you how to use these designs to make your own projects. Part I includes information about traditional American patchwork with some interesting facts about the history of patchwork design. It then goes on to teach the basic technique—how to make the stitch, how to read the graphs, and more. It lists the important terms and the supplies you will need for your work.

Part II is devoted to the designs. Each one is a single-block design meant to be used alone or in groups, with or without borders and/or margins. A full-size color-coded chart and a black-and-white photograph are given for each design. There are also color photographs of all the designs in the color section and on the front and back covers. All of these are well-known block designs that you have often seen in traditional quilts. In fact, for

many designs a museum source is given; a quilt incorporating that particular design is on display at that museum.

Part III consists of the projects. These are line drawings that show you some of the many ways you can use a block design in groups or alone, with or without borders and/or margins to make pillows, pictures, and other items. Exact stitch counts are given, as well as the sizes of proposed projects, both in inches and centimeters. The line drawings shown are very useful as guidelines to designing your own work.

In Part IV you are given the opportunity to choose any block design from Part II and change its pattern to suit your taste—not simply colors, but the entire pattern. One person might choose a bright calico print for a Le Moyne Star block design, while another might choose a pretty paisley. The block design would be the same for both, but the looks would be very different. The guidelines I have given in Part IV make the task of changing the patterns a relatively easy one to perform, and the ability to change patterns this way greatly increases your opportunities to be creative.

For those of you who like the challenge of creating your own block designs, a good deal of useful information and many helpful diagrams have been included in Part V to help you.

For beginners, the fun of this book may be in the fact that your time and effort are put into the design itself. Once you've established the basics, and it won't take you long to do that, your mind will be swimming with design possibilities. My mind is constantly seeing new design combinations, and so will yours.

PART 1

THE CRAFT

The combination of counted cross-stitch and traditional American patchwork is a natural. Patchwork is based on a variety of geometric shapes, most of which are easily adaptable to counted cross-stitch because of the nature of the cloth used to stitch. Evenweave fabric is ideal for developing a patchwork design in stitchery. The added bonus is that with counted cross-stitch you are able to develop pattern within each geometric shape.

About Traditional American Patchwork

It is not known exactly when quilting first began. We do know, however, that the Crusaders brought back quilted clothing from the Middle East, thus introducing quilting to the Western world. Women of all social classes began to work at quilting frames, and have been doing so ever since.

Throughout the English countryside quilting was routine. In the evenings, after the everyday chores were finished, young girls learned to quilt from their mothers. During her growing years before marriage, each girl made thirteen quilts. The first designs were simple ones; as the girl grew older, more complicated designs were attempted. The thirteenth quilt was called the Bride's Quilt. This one, saved for the last, was the most accomplished and elaborate of the baker's dozen.

When the first settlers came to this land, quilts were among the articles they brought. The living conditions in the new homeland dictated a change in the art and craft of quilt making. After a while, the first quilts that were brought to America wore out and had to be patched. Eventually, they were patched to a point where there were more patches than there was quilt. Scraps were saved to be pieced together to make meager bed coverings. So evolved the Crazy Quilt, the oldest known design in patchwork. No scrap of fabric was wasted in the Crazy Quilt; pieces fit together whichever way they fell. Quilting had evolved into patch quilting—a meager beginning for what is now thought of as a highly developed craft.

By 1750 the patchwork quilt had come into its own. Everyone had a scrap bag. America's women were cutting geometric shapes out of their saved scraps and piecing coverlet tops for quilts. After

seeing our pioneer mothers' quilts in museums, antique shops, and books, I can only marvel at their geometric genius. Their lack of formal schooling in math certainly had no adverse effect on the quality of their designs.

Because it was far too expensive to finish the quilt unless it was certain that it would be used, these coverlet tops were quilted only before an imminent marriage. The quilting bee became a social event at the time a young girl became engaged. Friends and neighbors came from the surrounding area and quilted all the coverlets for the bride to be. It might very well be that the engagement parties and bridal showers of today are the outgrowths of these social events.

After 1771, expensive imported fabrics began to come into America quite steadily. In wealthier homes quilts were made of fine linen, calico, chintz, cotton cambric, and gingham. In 1793 the cotton gin was invented and it was to completely change America's cloth industry. Prices of cloth began to go down and most women were able to purchase cloth by the length at the dry goods store. By 1850 the days of the scrap bag quilt were finished. More and more women planned their designs and pieced their quilts from purchased cloth. By 1870 the Crazy Quilt had emerged into one of design, color, and beauty. No home was without at least one elaborate quilt. Some of these quilts, which are now museum pieces with which we are all familiar, contain more than four thousand pieces.

Patchwork quilts are a picture portrayal of a two-hundred-year-old segment of America's home life. The subject matter and naming of quilts are no less significant topics for discussion than are the patchwork designs themselves. Occupations, religion, politics, nature, and social activities all played a part in the designing and naming of quilt patterns. The quilts were given charming names, and I have decided to use these in the book wherever possible to help keep those efforts alive.

The Star was, and still is, the most popular of all patterns. Anywhere you will find a collection of quilts today, you can be sure that you will find some variation of the Star pattern. The eight-pointed star has it's roots in the Le Moyne Star pattern. The Le Moyne brothers, Jean Baptiste being the younger, founded New Orleans in 1718. After the Louisiana Purchase in 1803, this star pattern found its way from New Orleans to New England. There it was renamed Lemon Star, probably because the New England housewife had an easier time pronouncing Lemon than she did Le Moyne, or possibly because these New England ladies wanted nothing to do with anything French.

It has long been wondered how, in days of limited travel, so many quilts, bearing not only the same pattern but the same name, managed to appear in both the West and East coasts of this country. Of course, one pattern could have been designed in one area, and, by chance, an identical pattern designed in another, but it is unlikely that both would have been given the same name. We do know that neighboring women exchanged patterns; perhaps peddlers purchased or bartered patterns, exchanging them with fellow peddlers along the way. It seems likely that quilt patterns could have traveled from one end of the country to the other in this sort of a relay.

The religious aspect of life brought us other star patterns, such as Star of Bethlehem, Christmas Star, and Blazing Star. Religion also brought us Joseph's Coat of Many Colors, Cross and Crown, and Tree of Life. From nature came names such as Bear's Paw, Goose in the Pond, Wild Goose Chase, and all the flower patterns—Autumn Leaves, Cactus Rose, North Carolina Lily, and Lazy Daisy.

Work was the major function of anyone's day and inspired by everyday tasks were names like Monkey Wrench, Pincushion, and Windmill. Last on the list of literally thousands of names (and for obvious reasons) are those derived from recreational activities. The square dance was the best known form of fun and from it comes Hands All Around.

Are we really to believe that women of those times had no interest in the politics of American life? Their quilts say otherwise. As examples we have Clay's Choice, Burgoyne Surrounded, Nelson's Victory, and Union Square. As a matter of fact, it was at a quilting bee that Susan B. Anthony gave her first political talk on equal rights.

Three historic quilt patterns have been named after famous women—Queen Charlotte's Crown, Dolly Madison's Star, and Mrs. Cleveland's Choice. In thinking about these we can see significant changes in America's history. Queen Charlotte, the last Queen of our thirteen original colonies, was the wife of George III. Her patch represents the end of a monarchy for America. During Dolly Madison's time, the White House was completely burned. It is said that before she fled to Virginia to safety, she took The Declaration of Independence and Gilbert Stuart's famous painting of George Washington with her. She was the leading lady of her day and appropriately was honored with a star pattern. It was seventy-five years later before quilt makers chose another woman to honor. At the age of twenty-two, a lovely young Frances Folsom came to the White House as the bride of Grover Cleveland. At a time when women's choices were just beginning to expand, she was honored with Mrs. Cleveland's Choice. Crown, Star, and Choice—a depiction of three changing eras.

The year 1880 seems to mark the end of an era of patchwork quilting. Women were becoming more independent and were gaining new economic status. Also, by this time, spreads and coverlets could easily be purchased. We did not hear from patchwork again for many years.

The first revival came in the 1930s and no one really knows why. Some say it was due to the Depression. Without extra money to spend perhaps women turned to patchwork quilting as an inexpensive, creative outlet.

Today we are at the height of another revival. I would venture a guess that this one has nothing to do with lack of money and a lot to do with the Industrial Age and our need (as well as the spare time) to create handcrafted pieces. All the supplies and sources are there for us to choose. Certainly we do not have the extra work of spinning and dyeing our own cloth. We do not need to hunt very far to find the right color or the proper pattern.

If you have the need to create, my hope is that this book will help fill part of that need. Your choices are numerous. You can recreate the designs exactly as seen in the book, change any of the colors, change any of the patterns, or design your own counted cross-stitch patchwork.

About Counted Cross-Stitch

Counted cross-stitch is one of the easiest of the needlework arts to learn. It starts with a simple × stitched with embroidery thread on evenweave fabric. The × is repeated many times and a pattern is formed by the changing of embroidery thread colors.

GATHERING YOUR MATERIALS

Often stamped-on-fabric embroidery patterns incorporate the cross-stitch, but these are not to be confused with true counted cross-stitch work. With these stamped backgrounds it is often difficult to find the exact corners of the stitch, which makes it difficult to keep the work even. For this reason true counted cross-stitch is done on an *evenweave fabric*, such as *Aida* (pronounced like the opera) cloth, the squares of which are very easy to see. Aida cloth is one hundred percent cotton and has the look of graph paper—a small even grid with tiny holes in the corners. With this kind of fabric, the work will always be even and in line. In counted cross-stitch you do not fill in the background. While there are many other evenweave fabrics available, for beginners I recommend Aida cloth. This does not mean that your work will not turn out beautifully with Aida. Aida cloth is used by all the professionals probably because it works up so easily and looks good. It comes in a wide variety of colors, such as white, ivory, pink, light blue, gold, yellow, beige, black, royal blue, and pistachio, and is also available in Christmas green and red. The color of the fabric you choose becomes an integral part of your design. It is left unstitched when used as a background and can also be part of the design itself if spaces are to be left unstitched.

The supplies used for counted cross-stitch are relatively inexpensive and fairly easy to find. All you need are a small, blunt tapestry needle, good embroidery thread, evenweave fabric, small scissors that are sharp, an embroidery hoop, good lighting, and a comfortable chair.

Aida cloth is available in sizes 8, 11, 14, and 18. (This means that there will be 8, 11, 14, and 18 stitches respectively to the inch.) All of the basic designs in this book were made using #14 Aida cloth, but instructions are given for #11 as well.

Other recommended evenweave fabrics are:

Hardanger: 22 stitch count; 100% cotton; available in many colors.

Dublin: 25 stitch count; 100% linen; available in some colors.

Linen: 32 stitch count; 100% linen; available in white and cream.

Klosters: 7 stitch count; 60% rayon, 40% cotton; available in beige; has a very soft and earthy look.

Floba: 18 stitch count; 30% linen, 70% viscose; available in oatmeal.

All of the fabrics listed are hand washable, which is a distinct advantage. Aida was chosen for the designs in this book because it is the most well known, is available in more colors, and has the widest variety of stitch counts. Hardanger can be used for any project you might want to make that would require a good deal of subtle shading. The smaller the stitch, the more you can shade. Klosters, on the other hand, is not good for shading, but, because of its soft and earthy look, bold single designs can be stitched very nicely. I used Klosters to stitch the single Eight-Pointed Star on the color page of finished projects. Notice how much bigger that single-block design works up on Klosters. Although Floba has an 18 stitch count, it really becomes 9 stitches to the inch when stitched over two threads, as is done with any linen. The single Pieced Star on the color page was stitched on Floba.

You will find all kinds of linen available, and they are lovely for napkins, tablecloths, and any household linens you choose. There are many other fabrics available to you, and I would suggest you go to your local needlework supply shop and ask to see and feel the various fabrics.

Working on evenweave linen, there are no set holes to see. You must stitch by the grain of the fabric. The cross-stitch is worked over two threads both ways. (See Figure 4.) In the beginning the thread count is not easy to follow, but give it a chance. Soon your eyes will become accustomed to seeing the thread count much more easily.

In addition to the evenweave fabric you will need:

A tapestry needle: A blunt, short needle, sizes 24 or 26 are good, unless you are using a coarser fabric.

Embroidery thread: Six-strand cotton embroidery floss comes in a myriad of colors and is easy to purchase. D.M.C. embroidery floss has been used in the color coding of this book. For #14 Aida cloth work with two strands of a six-strand piece of cotton embroidery floss. For #11 Aida use three strands of a six-strand piece. Crewel wool and Persian yarn are lovely on evenweave wool and other coarse fabrics. You might also consider using Danish flower thread, which is a thicker thread. One strand of it equals two strands of cotton floss.

Scissors: A sharp pair of embroidery scissors, with which you should never cut paper.

Embroidery hoop: Plastic or wooden, round or oval, with good screw tension, a good size for these individual designs is 5 or 6 inches.

Good light: Save your eyes.

A comfortable chair: And I'm not kidding.

Cross-stitch supplies are available at art needlework shops all over the world. If you do, however, find that some of the supplies are not available in your particular area, you are invited to write to me at this address:

P.O. Drawer RRR
Southampton, New York 11968.

A WORD ABOUT CHARTED DESIGNS

Counted cross-stitch is usually worked from a graph, or charted design. The charts in this book are not worked on a graph, but do utilize a graph concept. Rows of symbols are lined up horizontally and vertically. Just as each symbol on a graph represents a single stitch, each symbol on these charts represents a single stitch. In this way confusing graph lines are not necessary. Figure 1 shows a charted design. The × represents one color and the ○ another. On a graph, a space to be left unstitched would be symbolized by a blank space, but here it is symbolized by a dot.

```
OO··OO··OO··OO··OO··OO··OO
OO··OO··OO··OO··OO··OO··OO
··XX··XX··XX··XX··XX··XX··
··XX··XX··XX··XX··XX··XX··
OO··OO··OO··OO··OO··OO··OO
OO··OO··OO··OO··OO··OO··OO
··XX··XX··XX··XX··XX··XX··
··XX··XX··XX··XX··XX··XX··
OO··OO··OO··OO··OO··OO··OO
OO··OO··OO··OO··OO··OO··OO
··XX··XX··XX··XX··XX··XX··
··XX··XX··XX··XX··XX··XX··
OO··OO··OO··OO··OO··OO··OO
OO··OO··OO··OO··OO··OO··OO
··XX··XX··XX··XX··XX··XX··
··XX··XX··XX··XX··XX··XX··
OO··OO··OO··OO··OO··OO··OO
OO··OO··OO··OO··OO··OO··OO
··XX··XX··XX··XX··XX··XX··
··XX··XX··XX··XX··XX··XX··
OO··OO··OO··OO··OO··OO··OO
OO··OO··OO··OO··OO··OO··OO
```

Figure 1

Charted design with graph lines eliminated.

FINDING THE SIZE OF YOUR FINISHED PIECE

Before you purchase fabric, you must know the size your design will be when finished. There is a very simple way to figure this out in advance. Here is an example: If you are using fabric with a stitch count of 14 (this means there will be 14 stitches to the inch), and the stitched area of design is 56 stitches × 56 stitches, your design will be 4 inches (10 cm.) square. You arrive at this by dividing your design stitch count—56—by your fabric stitch count—14. The answer is 4, which means that your finished size will be 4 inches. Remember: Divide the count of your stitches in the design area by the count of your fabric.

PREPARING YOUR FABRIC

When purchasing your fabric, always allow for seam allowance and finishing and purchase a larger piece. Don't be skimpy. It's better to have too much than too little. I'd hate to run out of fabric with ninety-eight percent of my project finished. The slight extra cost is worth it.

Once you have your fabric, prepare it by hemming or taping the cut sides. This is so your piece will not ravel while you are working. (Keep in mind that tape sometimes comes off.) Locate the exact center of your fabric by folding it in half north to south, then in half east to west. Put a straight pin through this center corner lightly to keep the mark, but be careful not to damage the fabric. Place the fabric on your embroidery hoop and pull the fabric taut. The tighter, the better, for this makes for easy stitching. As you stitch, tighten your fabric as needed. Tighten the screw tension and keep it tight while working.

MAKING THE STITCH

You can make your first stitch at whatever point you choose. Study the graph and choose your starting point. Then you must locate this first stitch on your fabric. Find the center of the graph and count up and over on the graph until you have reached your chosen starting point. For example, let's say that this point is 8 stitches up and 4 stitches to the left of the center of the graph. Leaving your straight pin in the center of your fabric, count 8 stitches up and 4 stitches to the left of the straight pin. Use your threaded needle to count and start stitching right at that spot. Once you have 2 or 3 stitches done, recheck your count before taking the straight pin out.

The cross-stitch is quite simple to make. Bring the threaded needle up from the underside of the fabric through the lower left-hand corner of the square. Cross over diagonally and insert your needle in the upper right hand corner of the square, bringing it through to the underside again, as shown in Figure 2. It does not matter whether you make the first half of the cross from the lower left to the upper right, or from the lower right to the upper left, as long as you are consistent. Whichever way you choose, ALWAYS execute the first half of the cross-stitch in the same way. You may think this does not matter, since you really can't see a difference, but, if stitched at random, when light hits the finished project, a shadow will form in varying directions, which will detract from your design. Most Americans make their stitches from lower left to upper right, as shown in Figure 2. Europeans do exactly the opposite. In any case, finish the other half of the stitch by coming from the underside into the lower right-hand corner, crossing over diagonally, and going into the upper left-hand corner, as shown in Figure 3. (If you are working on an evenweave linen, refer to Figure 4.)

If you have never worked on counted cross-stitch before, practice. Take a small piece of fabric and place it on your hoop, keeping the fabric taut. The screw on the hoop should be to the left if you are right-handed and to the right if you are left-handed. Two o'clock or ten o'clock are good positions for the screw. This is done so that you do not get your thread tangled in the screw and also to help you remember which side of your work faces north. It is important that you always stitch with the top side of your work facing north, so that the first half of your cross-stitch always slants in the same direction. If your screw is always in the same place, you will automatically know which is the north side of your work. This is particularly important on the designs in this book, since they are all balanced. In other words, a design could be turned sideways and still look as though it were facing the right way. The length of your thread should be about 18 inches (45 cm.) long. Do not knot your work; it may look bumpy on the finished piece. Start by holding a small piece of thread on the underside of your work and stitching the first few stitches over it, as shown in Figure 5. Work some ×'s on your sample piece of fabric to get the feel. Work some stitches from right to left and from left to right. Move along north and south and stitch diagonally. Some embroiderers prefer to cross one complete stitch at a time. Others cross only half stitches in a line and

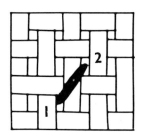

Figure 2
One half cross-stitch.

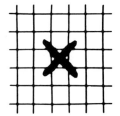

Figure 4

On evenweave linen, the cross is made over two threads.

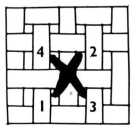

Figure 3
Full cross-stitch.

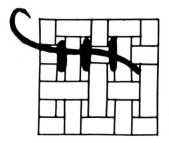

Figure 5
Underside of fabric.

then stitch back over them, crossing the other half. Either method works as long as you have a long row of one color, but, while there are some long continuous rows in these designs, most of them are patterns. This means that the colors change along the rows. For these it will be easier if you cross each stitch completely and watch the pattern form.

End your thread on your sample piece by weaving it in and out of a few stitches on the underside of your fabric. Cut off all ends. Now change to another color. When moving a color from one place to another run it under some stitches on the underside of your fabric. Try not to run colors across the back for any more than a few stitches at a time. Avoid running a thread from one place to another on the underside of an area that will be left unstitched. These may very well show through to the right side of your fabric.

FINISHING YOUR WORK

Wash your work in lukewarm water and use a mild soap. Make sure you have rinsed well and do not ring out the fabric. Place wet work on a terry towel and roll the towel up. Press with your hands on the rolled towel to absorb the moisture. On the wrong side, immediately iron your piece over a padded surface. (Another dry folded terry towel is good.) When your piece is ironed properly, lay it on a clean flat surface and do not touch it until it is thoroughly dry. No matter how dry you think the work is after ironing, there is still moisture content in the fibers. Once thoroughly dry, your work is ready to mount.

If you are framing a picture, mount your work on a stiff piece of cardboard, Masonite, or a stretcher frame. It can be taped or stapled to the back side. Always make sure your backing has a white surface, if you are using a white or light fabric for your stitching, as the color might show through. Stretch your fabric as evenly as possible over the mounting board before taping or stapling. Evenweave fabrics are not hard to stretch, and you can probably do that yourself, before your project is framed.

A LIST OF TERMS

The following is a list of the terms used throughout the rest of the book. These are terms you will need to become familiar with, so go over the list before you go on to the rest of the book and refer back to it from time to time.

Block: A group of geometric shapes, either the same or different, that together make a patchwork design. I call the designs in Part 2 one-block designs.

Shape: The forms—triangles, squares, hexagons, etc.—that when arranged together make up one block.

Pattern: The specific design used within a shape, such as flowers, checks, plaids, etc.

Border: A stitched design around the outer dimensions of a block or blocks.

Margin: An unstitched area of fabric around the block or blocks or around the outside area of the stitched border.

Piece or Finished Piece: The project in total, including all the blocks, borders, and margins.

PART 2

THE SINGLE-BLOCK DESIGNS

The following are forty-eight American patchwork block designs that I have adapted to counted cross-stitch. I'm sure you will enjoy these, just as I do, but don't be afraid to alter them or change the patterns—something you will be taught how to do in Part 4.

All of these stitched block designs are presented in the same way. Read the following information so that you will be familiar with the format.

Sizes: The size given refers to spaces across by spaces down. For example, the Autumn Leaves size is given as 62 × 62. This means that it is 62 spaces across and 62 spaces down. Keep in mind that this refers to the stitched area only.

Charts: For each of the forty-eight designs given there is a chart. Each symbol on the chart represents 1 stitch and a dot represents 1 space left unstitched. A symbol change represents a color change, so, if there are four different symbols on the chart, this means there are to be four colors in the block. A color code, matching symbols to D.M.C. embroidery floss colors, is given for each chart. Arrows pointing toward the center of each chart are an aid to finding the exact center. Draw an imaginary line from these arrows across the chart. The exact center of the chart is the point at which the two lines intersect.

Color Codes: The charts have been coded to D.M.C. embroidery floss colors, which are made in France, but which are readily available in this country. The color codes list the symbols used in the chart, the names of the colors, and the D.M.C. number floss that I used.

Photographs: To give you a better idea of how the finished design looks there is a black-and-white photograph of each design, right below the chart. The photograph of each block is fractionally smaller than the actual finished size (when done on #14 Aida).

General Instructions: A small paragraph pertaining to the particular design accompanies each one. Sometimes it deals with the history of the design, sometimes with the stitching, and sometimes both. In general, start stitching in the center of the block, unless otherwise instructed. It's a good idea to look for the repeat pattern, which is usually symbolized by the ● or ○ symbol. It is sometimes easier to start this way.

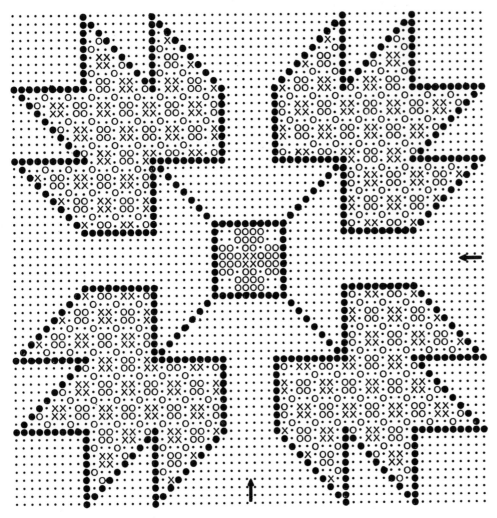

AUTUMN LEAVES

SIZE - 62 x 62
D.M.C. COLOR CODE

```
.  Unstitched
o  Red    817
x  Gold   783
●  Olive  3346
```

Start stitching in the center
part of this design. Work the
stems toward the leaves. Outline all the ●'s of each leaf
before stitching the pattern.

16

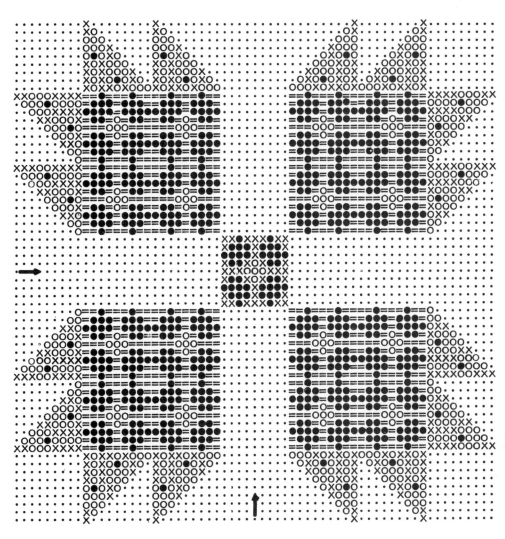

BEAR'S PAW

DUCK'S FOOT IN THE MUD

SIZE - 63 x 63
D.M.C. COLOR CODE

.	Unstitched
●	Brown 838
o	Yellow 725
=	Red 350
x	Salmon 352

Bear's Paw is the most common
name for this block. On Long
Island, it is known as Duck's
Foot in the Mud. Start stitching from the center.

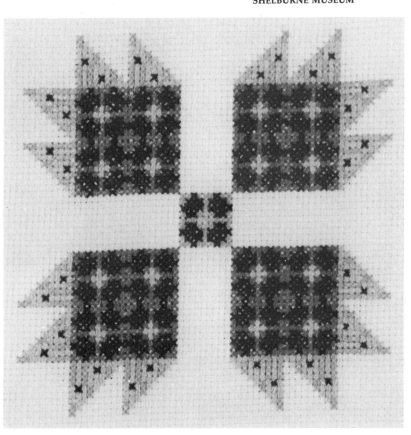

17

BLAZING STAR

STAR OF THE EAST

SIZE - 61 x 61
D.M.C. COLOR CODE

. Unstitched
o Dark Blue 797
● Red 600
x Med. Blue 798

An overall design which goes
on forever, growing out from
the center star.
Refer to Projects, Part III.

18

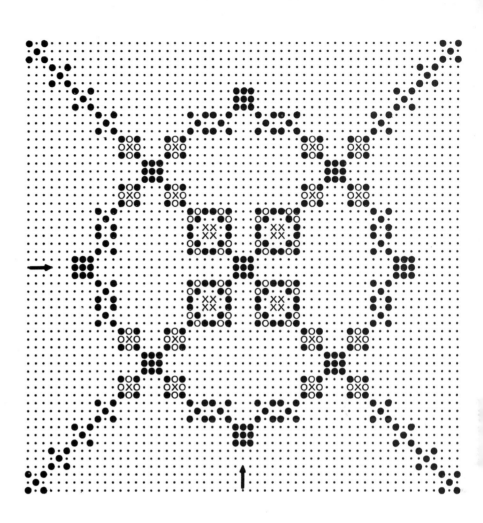

BURGOYNE SURROUNDED

SIZE – 57 x 57
D.M.C. COLOR CODE

. Unstitched
o Olive 3346
● Gold 781
x Wine 498

When made into a pillow, this very good overall pattern has a softer appearance than some bolder patchwork. An easy and fast project for beginners. Refer to Projects, Part III.

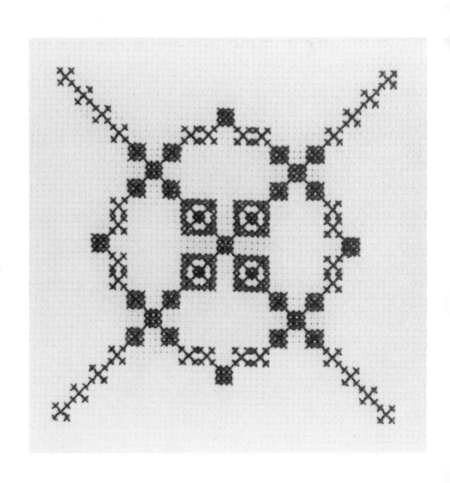

19

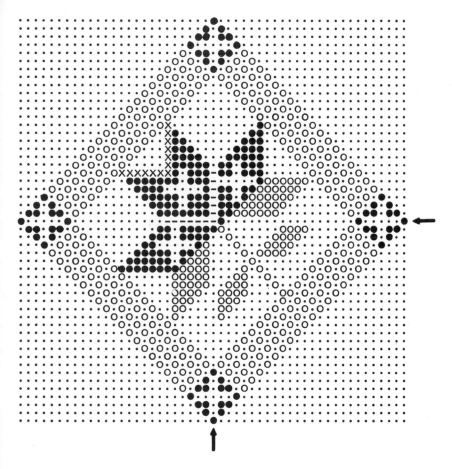

CACTUS ROSE

SIZE - 51 x 51
D.M.C. COLOR CODE

```
.    Unstitched
●    Red    817
o    Olive 3346
x    Red Half Cross \
-    Red Half Cross /
```

Cactus Rose is another flower pattern derived from the star shape. Many flower patterns originate from a star. Start at center of the flower, stem first.
Refer to Projects, Part III.

20

CHRISTMAS STAR

SIZE - 61 x 61
D.M.C. COLOR CODE

.	Unstitched	
o	Red	817
x	Mint	704
●	Pink	605

Star patterns far outnumber
other old patchwork patterns.
Christmas Star is a variation
of Star of Bethlehem. It is
best to begin from the center
of this block.
Refer to Projects, Part III.

COMPASS

SIZE - 59 x 59
D.M.C. COLOR CODE

. Unstitched
x Dark Green 699
o Yellow   444
● Orange   350

The Compass block offers a
fantastic assortment of design possibilities, of which
this is only one example. It
is also known as Four Winds.
Stitch from the center.
Refer to Projects, Part III.

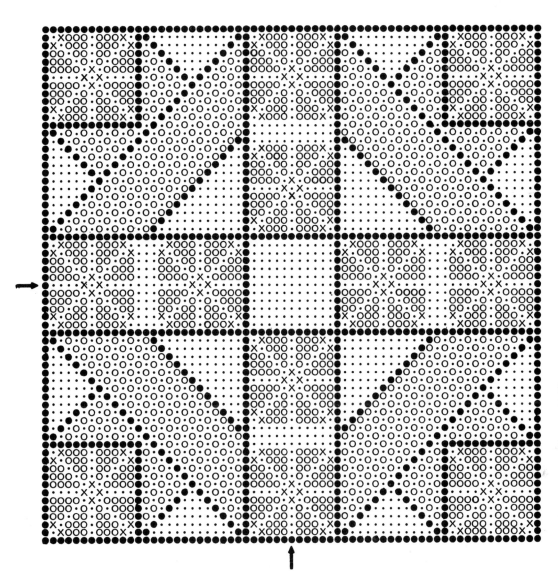

CROSS AND CROWN

SIZE - 65 x 65
D.M.C. COLOR CODE

.   Unstitched
o   Purple 550
●   Red   817
x   Gold   725

Many old quilt patterns have biblical names. Considering the influence of religion on American history, this would not seem unusual. Begin to stitch by outlining all ●'s, making this design easier to follow.

23

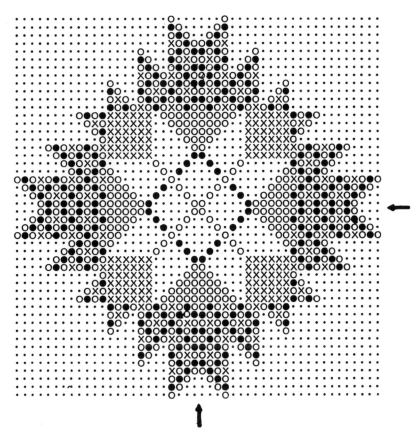

DELECTABLE MOUNTAINS

SIZE - 65 x 65
D.M.C. COLOR CODE

.	Unstitched	
o	Blue	519
●	Blue	517
x	Green	734

This block usually starts at
the center of a quilt. The
mountains surround the center
and continue until a project
is as large as you choose.
Refer to Projects, Part III.

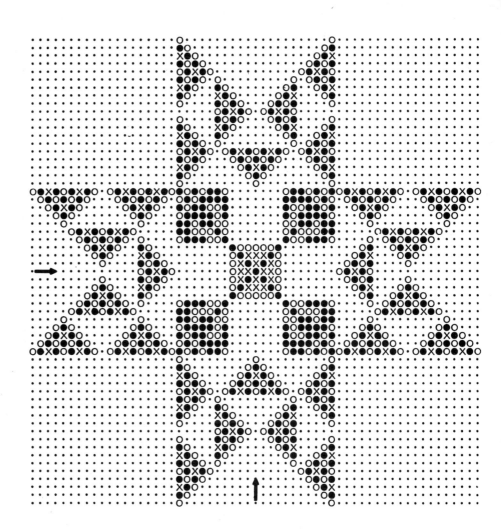

DOLLY MADISON'S STAR

SIZE - 59 x 59
D.M.C. COLOR CODE

.	Unstitched	
●	Olive	3346
o	Yellow	725
x	Rust	919

The center square of this star is to be stitched first. Dolly Madison is one of 3 famous women for whom a patchwork design was named. Usually sewn in red, white, and blue.

25

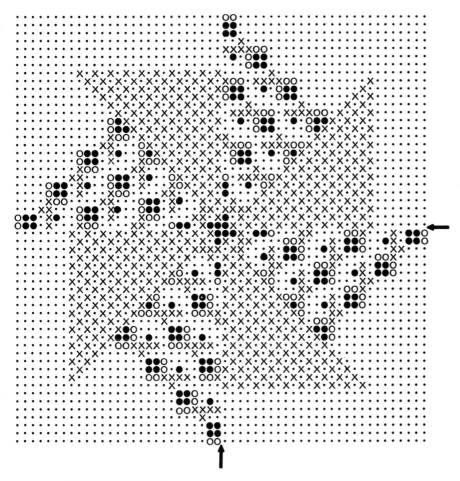

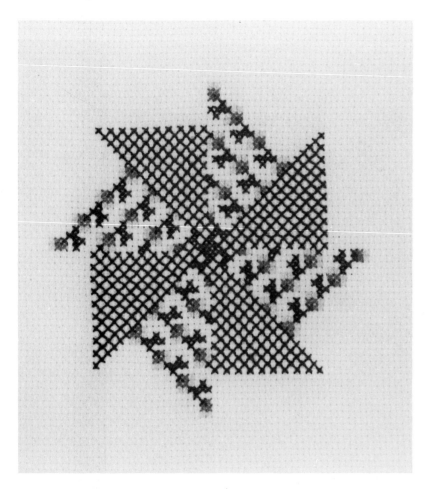

DOUBLE PINWHEEL

SIZE - 54 x 54
D.M.C. COLOR CODE

.	Unstitched	
●	Red	817
x	Green	501
o	Salmon	353

By charting either the cross
hatch pattern, or the flower
separately, you can stitch a
single Pinwheel. By alternating the 2, another design can
be achieved. A very easy
project for beginners.
Refer to Projects, Part III.

26

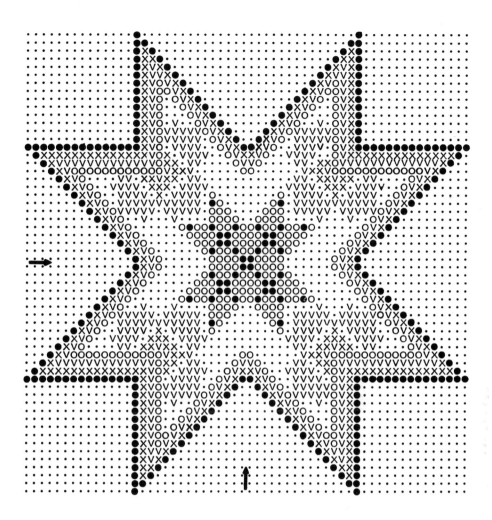

EIGHT-POINTED STAR

SIZE - 58 x 58
D.M.C. COLOR CODE

.	Unstitched	
●	Blue	336
o	Mauve	224
v	Blue	322
x	Rust	221

Of all the patchwork designs none can compare to the star pattern. There are so many a design book could be written just on stars. Start by outlining the star.
Refer to Projects, Part III.

FALLING STAR

SIZE - 62 x 62
D.M.C. COLOR CODE

```
.    Unstitched
●    Wine    915
o    Blue    517
x    Olive   3346
```

At about 1800 Falling Star was a favorite in New England and Pennsylvania. Start to stitch at any corner. A relatively easy block to stitch.
Refer to Projects, Part III.

28

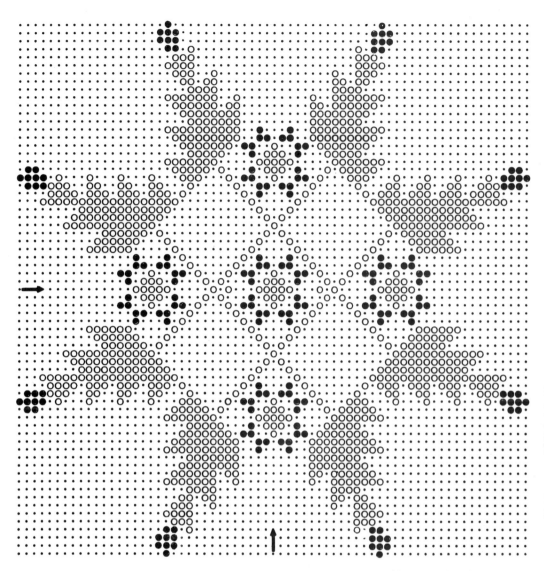

FEATHERED STAR

CALIFORNIA STAR

SIZE - 67 x 67
D.M.C. COLOR CODE

.   Unstitched
●   Red   498
o   Blue   796

One of the most beautiful star
patterns ever designed, and
one of the most complicated to
quilt. Start to stitch at the
center. Four of these stars
together with the small star
pattern in each corner make a
very effective project.

29

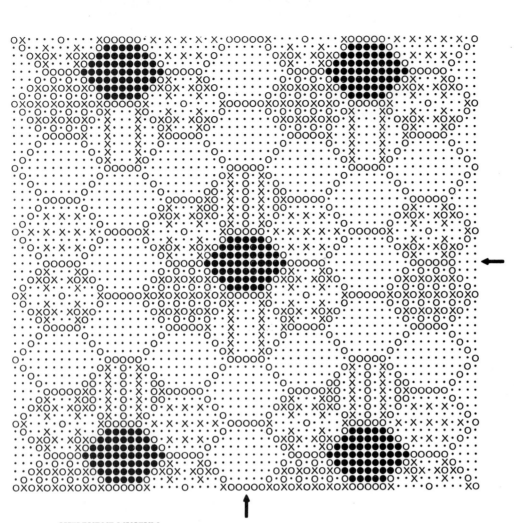

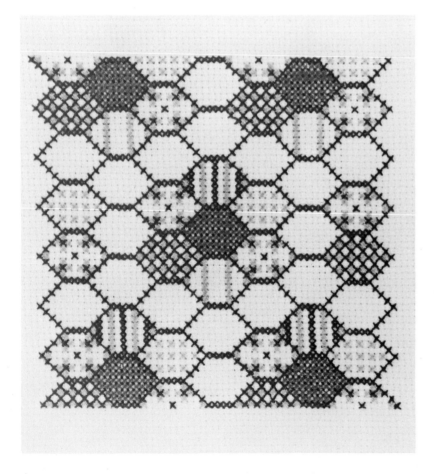

FLOWER GARDEN

SIZE - 61 x 57
D.M.C. COLOR CODE

.   Unstitched
o   Blue   336
●   Rust   221
x   Mauve 224

This entire design is comprised of hexagons. The center of the flower is usually solid in color, the petals various patterns, and white becomes a path around the garden. This is an overall pattern based on the Mosaic block. Refer to Projects, Part III.

30

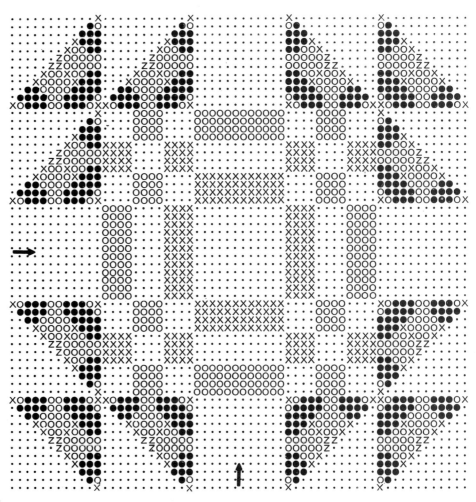

GOOSE IN THE POND

YOUNG MAN'S FANCY

SIZE - 60 x 60
D.M.C. COLOR CODE

.	Unstitched	
●	Brown	801
o	Turquoise	993
z	Yellow	444
x	Wine	915

A block which seems to be of
Massachusetts origin, dating
back to 1810. Surprisingly,
it has been found in many
parts of the country carrying
the same name.
Refer to Projects, Part III.

31

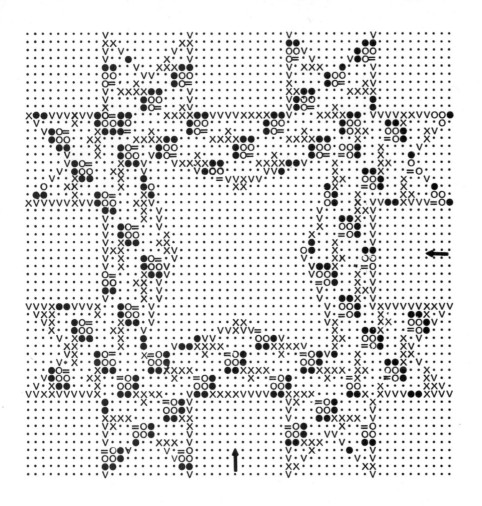

HANDS ALL AROUND

SIZE - 56 x 56
D.M.C. COLOR CODE

.	Unstitched	
v	Lavender	210
●	Purple	550
o	Lilac	208
=	Gold	726
x	Green	704

Hands All Around represents a circle of square dancers joining hands. It is one of those rare quilt patterns that takes it's name from a form of recreation.

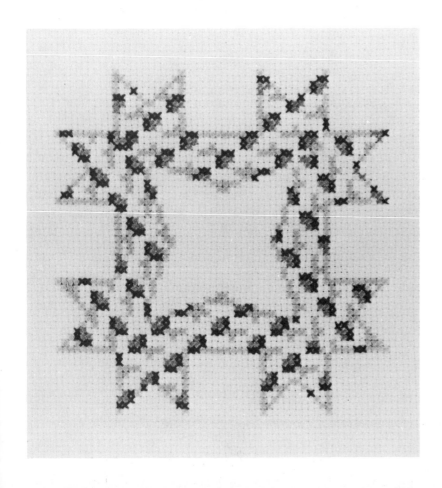

32

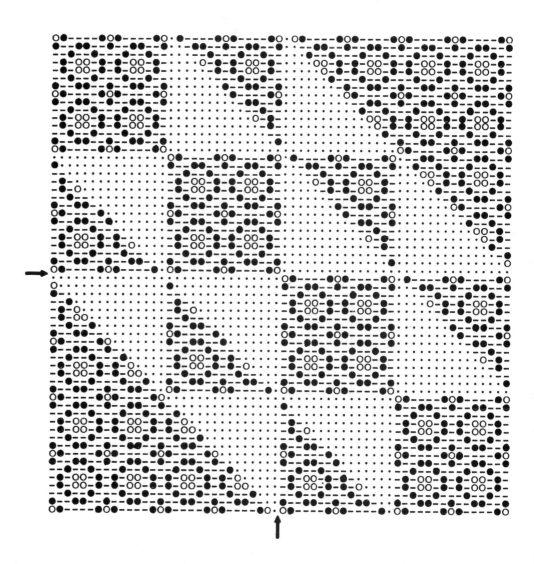

HOVERING HAWKS

SIZE - 60 x 60
D.M.C. COLOR CODE

.   Unstitched
=   Pink   605
●   Green   702
o   Red   600

This block has been reversed.
The design is unstitched and
the background stitched.
Choose another pattern and try
to design your own block this
way.

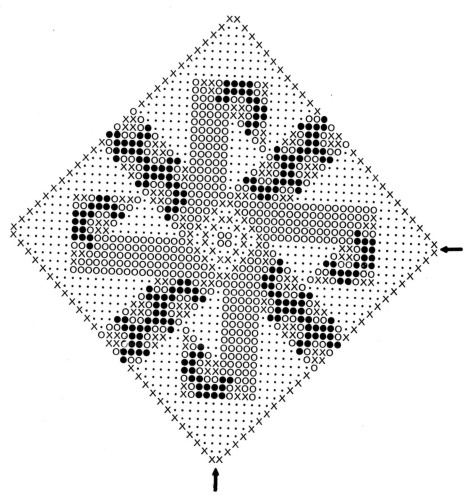

JACK-IN-THE-BOX

SIZE - 56 x 56
D.M.C. COLOR CODE

.   Unstitched
o   Bittersweet 350
x   Gold   783
●   Green   368

A perfect small pattern to be
used for making coasters.   An
initial can be stitched in the
center. Simply leave unstitched
as much of the center design as
needed, and use an initial instead.

34

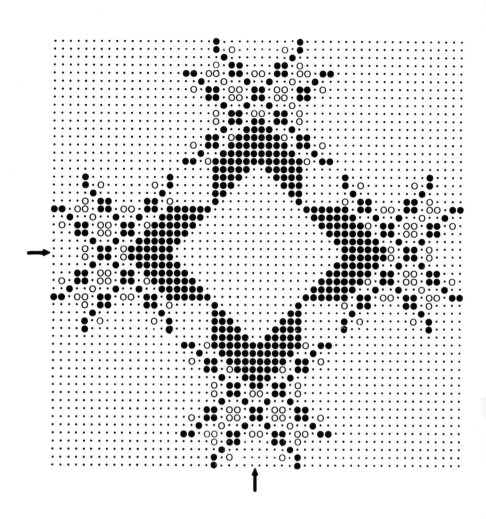

JACKSON STAR

SIZE - 54 x 54
D.M.C. COLOR CODE

.   Unstitched
●   Red   817
o   Blue   792

An initial in the center of
this design is also very effective in cross-stitch. It
is simple to work and pretty
framed. If framed, make sure
to leave a margin.
Refer to Projects, Part III.

JOSEPH'S COAT OF MANY COLORS

SIZE - 55 x 55
D.M.C. COLOR CODE

.	Unstitched	
x	Lavender	210
v	Orange	741
z	Green	704
=	Yellow	444
o	Red	817
●	Blue	820

A beautiful design to stitch,
using the colors of a rainbow.
However, it is not a pattern
for a beginner to try. This
patch used every piece of fabric
in the scrap bag.

36

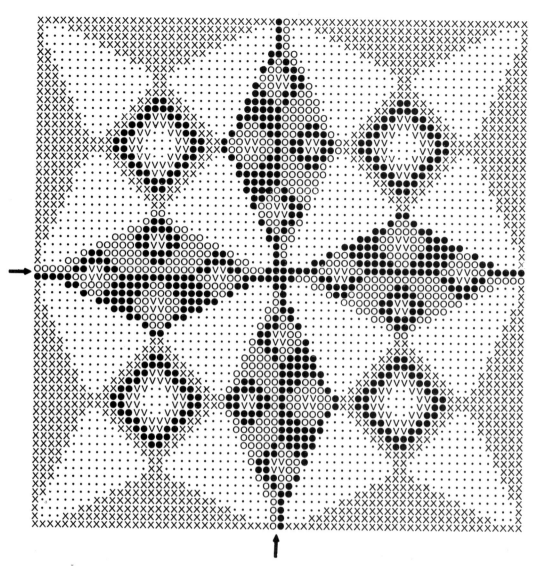

KALEIDOSCOPE

SIZE - 64 x 64
D.M.C. COLOR CODE

x   Lavender 210
●   Purple   550
o   Magenta 600
v   Pink   605
.   Unstitched

No other name could be more
appropriate. Not a project
for beginners, unless you
must have a real challenge.

37

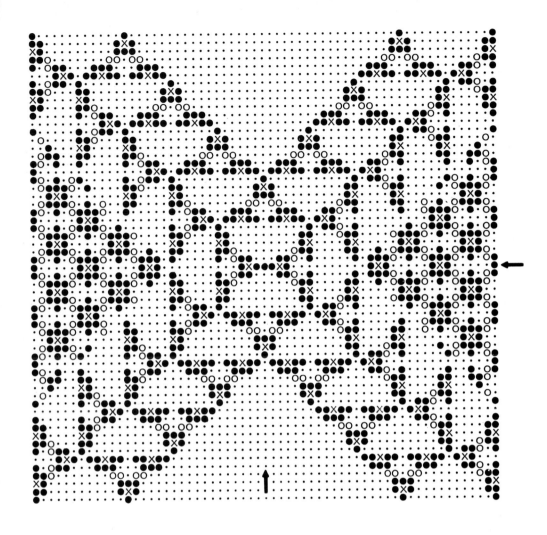

LADY OF THE LAKE

SIZE - 61 x 59
D.M.C. COLOR CODE

.	Unstitched	
●	Red	600
o	Green	699
x	Yellow	726

First seen in Vermont shortly after 1810. Lady of the Lake, named after Sir Walter Scott's poem, has never been known by any other name. Start in the center. If you choose, add a fourth color making the shapes true triangles.

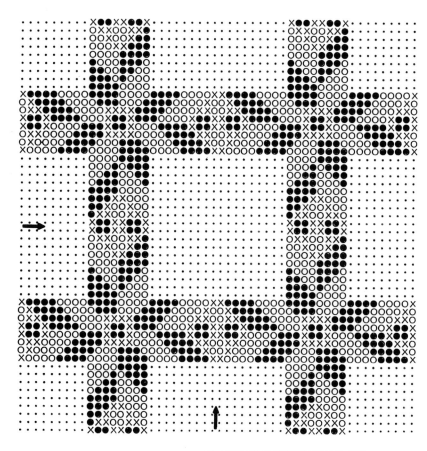

LAZY DAISY

SIZE - 52 x 52
D.M.C. COLOR CODE

```
.   Unstitched
●   Blue   517
o   Blue   519
x   Green  734
```

By enlarging the shapes within
this block you can stitch a pattern against a solid very effect-
ively. Have fun designing your
own block in this manner.

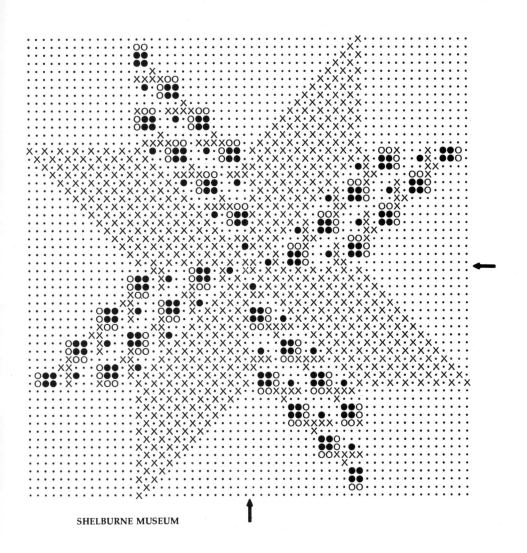

LE MOYNE STAR

```
SIZE - 58 x 58
D.M.C. COLOR CODE

.   Unstitched
o   Gold    783
●   Red     817
x   Olive  3346
```

A star named after the Le Moyne
brothers, Jean Baptiste being
the younger. In New England it
is called Lemon Star, probably
a name more easily pronounced.
A very easy block to stitch.

40

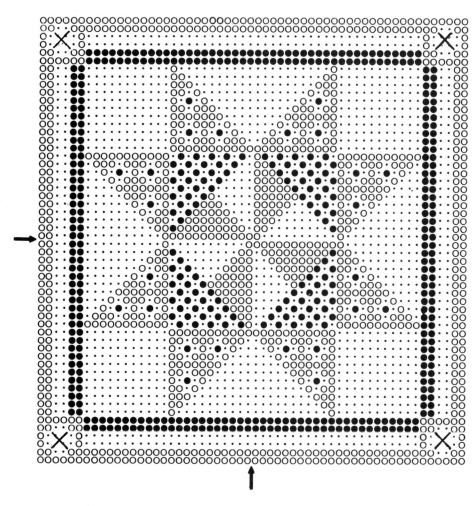

LONE STAR

OHIO STAR

SIZE - 56 x 56
D.M.C. COLOR CODE

. Unstitched
o Red   498
● Blue 796

Another striking star pattern
including the border. Stitch
together in twos. The right
border of this block becomes
the left border of the next.

41

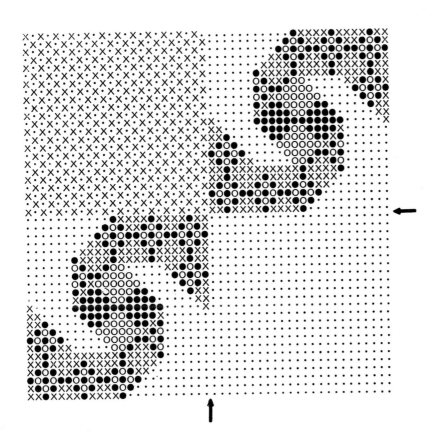

MONKEY WRENCH

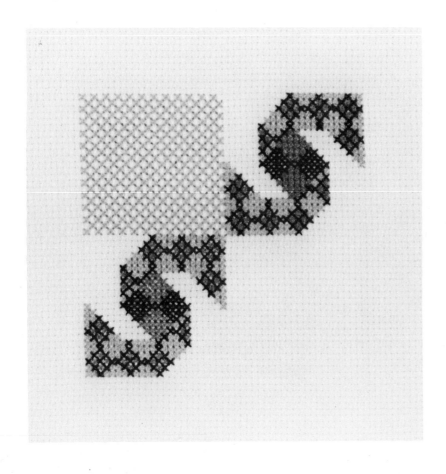

SIZE - 48 x 46
D.M.C. COLOR CODE

.	Unstitched	
o	Bittersweet	350
●	Brown	801
x	Coral	352

Monkey Wrench is an overall pattern. If you choose, use the cross hatch pattern on the unstitched one-quarter of this block. I did not, so when the blocks are put together, you get alternating rows of cross hatch and unstitched area.
Refer to Projects, Part III.

42

MOSAIC

SIZE - 60 x 60
D.M.C. COLOR CODE

.	Unstitched	
●	Olive	3346
o	Pink	605
v	Green	704
x	Pink	603
z	Gold	725

The Mosaic patch is sewn together using only one shape.
The hexagon forms an overall
pattern from the center and
grows out.
Refer to Projects, Part III.

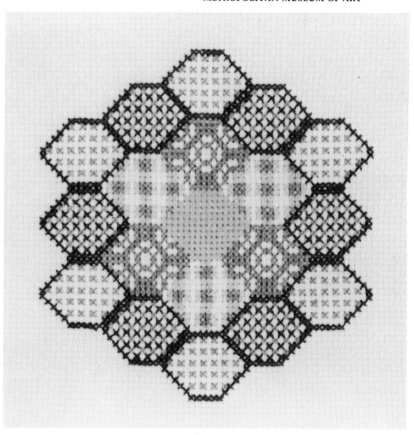

43

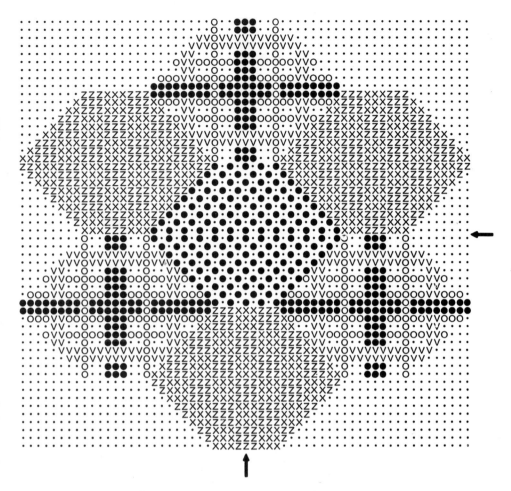

SHELBURNE MUSEUM

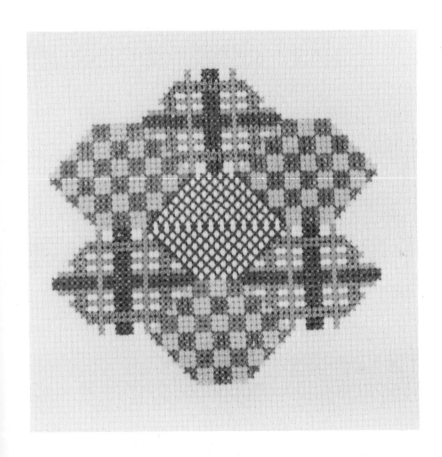

MOSAIC VARIATION

SIZE - 59 x 59
D.M.C. COLOR CODE

.	Unstitched	
o	Med. Salmon	352
●	Bittersweet	350
x	Lt. Salmon	353
v	Green	605
z	Dk. Salmon	351

There is an unlimited variety
of ways the hexagon shape can
be used. See Mosaic and Flower
Garden for two other possibilities.
Refer to Projects, Part III.

44

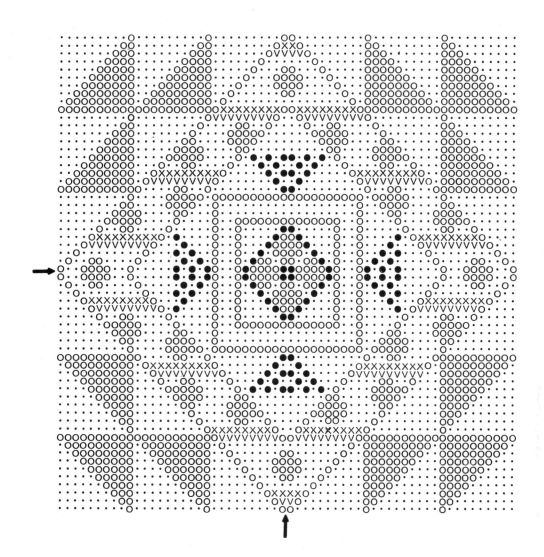

MRS. CLEVELAND'S CHOICE

SIZE - 60 x 60
D.M.C. COLOR CODE

.	Unstitched	
o	Lavender	209
●	Green	702
x	Green	702
v	Green	702
x	Half Cross	
v	Half Cross	

President Cleveland's wife is
one of three well-known women
for whom quilt patches have
been named. Note- the x symbol and v symbol are half cross-
stitches. Together they form a
herringbone look.

45

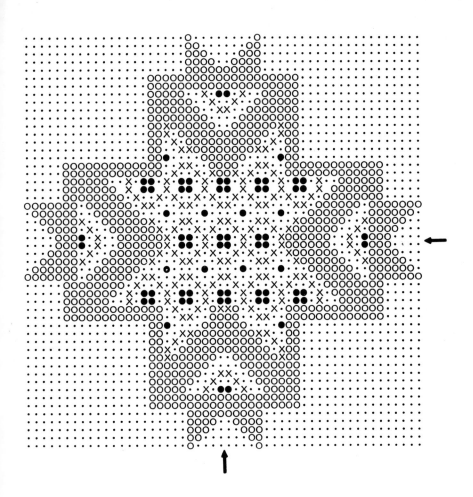

MY MOTHER'S STAR

SIZE - 50 x 50
D.M.C. COLOR CODE

.	Unstitched	
●	Bittersweet	350
o	Rust	919
x	Turquoise	993

A very pretty design, easy to
have fun with if you choose to
change the pattern of the star.

46

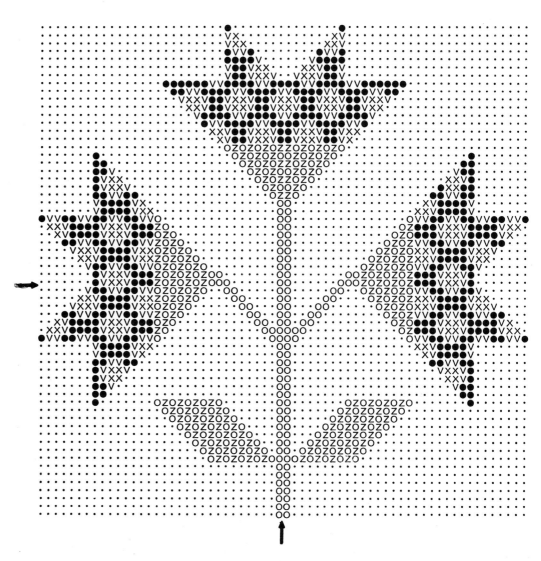

NORTH CAROLINA LILY

SIZE - 64 x 64
D.M.C. COLOR CODE

.	Unstitched	
●	Red	817
v	Pink	605
x	Gold	725
o	Green	699
z	Green	368

Most all lily and tulip shapes
originate from the star. If you
would like an open-work look in
this block, omit the z symbol.
Refer to Projects, Part III.

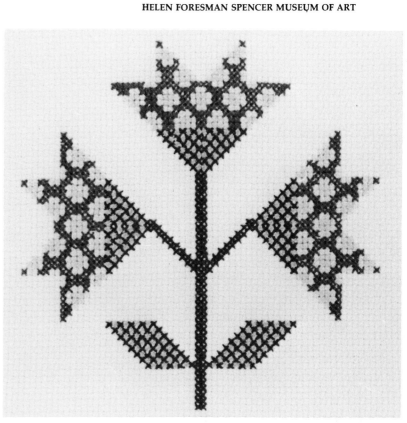

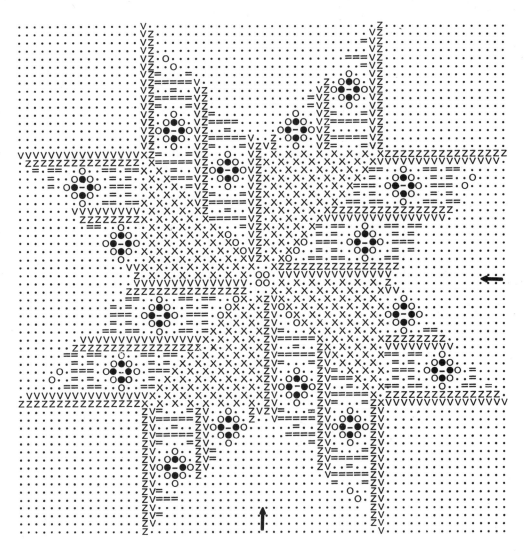

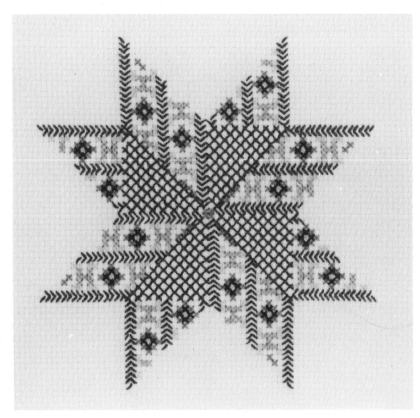

PIECED STAR

SIZE - 64 x 64
D.M.C. COLOR CODE

.	Unstitched	
o	Dark Salmon	349
=	Light Coral	352
●	Brown	801
-	Gold	742
x	Olive	3346
v	Olive	3346
v	Half Cross	
z	Half Cross	
z	Olive	3346

Another quilting pattern which was intended to use up all the scraps in the bag. Notice the v and z symbol are both olive and half cross-stitches, which form a herringbone look.
Refer to Projects, Part III.

48

PINCUSHION

SIZE - 53 x 53
D.M.C. COLOR CODE

.	Unstitched	
x	Green	470
●	Wine	915
o	Blue	792

If alternating rows of this
block are left unstitched,
another pleasing effect will
be achieved.

49

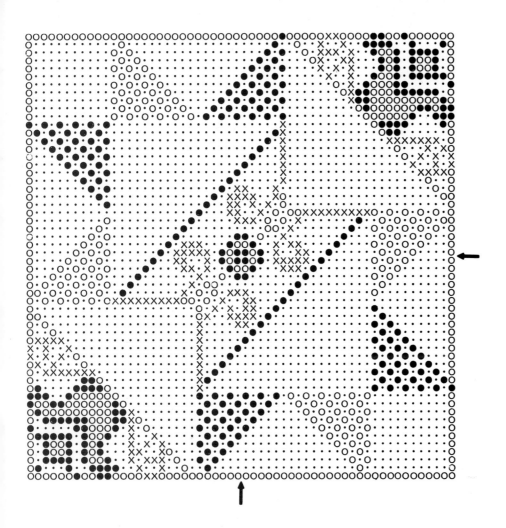

QUEEN CHARLOTTE'S CROWN

SIZE - 56 x 56
D.M.C. COLOR CODE

. Unstitched
o Blue   793
● Red   915
x Green 3346

America's last Queen was Queen
Charlotte, wife of George III–
the first of three famous women
to have quilt patterns named
after them. See Dolly Madison's
Star and Mrs. Cleveland's Choice.

50

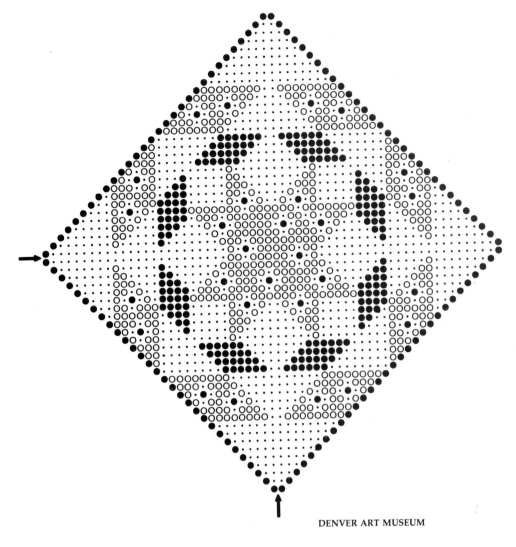

RING AROUND THE STAR

WINGED SQUARE

SIZE - 60 x 60
D.M.C. COLOR CODE

.   Unstitched
o   Blue   797
●   Green 702

This pattern is usually made entirely of diamond shapes and is not an easy quilting piece. However, it is an easy cross-stitch pattern of only 2 colors on an ivory ground.

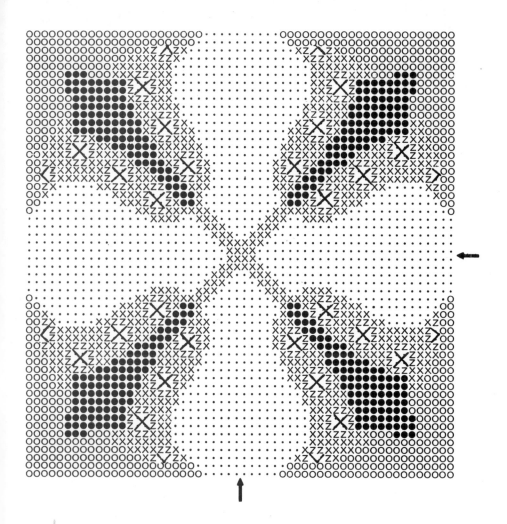

SLAVE BLOCK

SIZE - 56 x 56
D.M.C. COLOR CODE

.	Unstitched	
z	Lime Green	704
x	Dark Green	702
●	Hot Pink	603
o	Orange	741

This pattern is called Slave Block, as it was chiefly made by the slaves in the South.

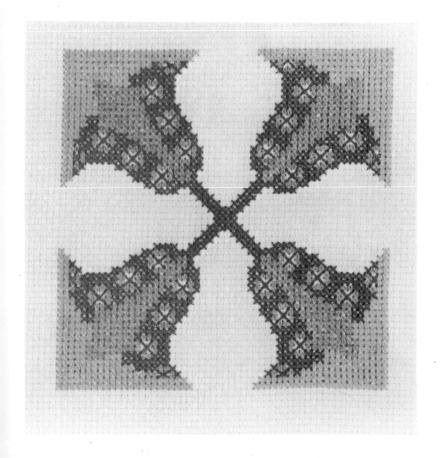

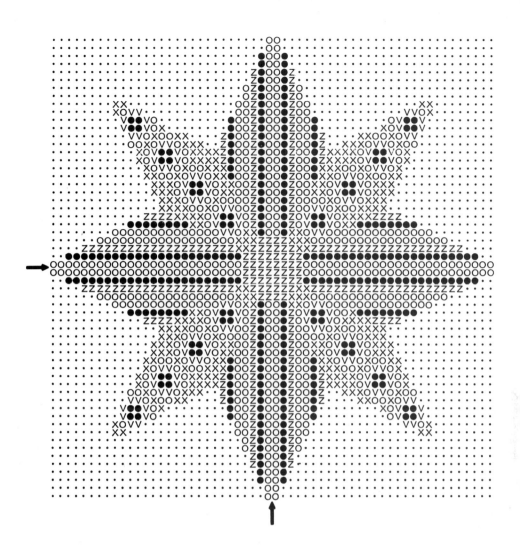

STAR FLOWER

SIZE - 58 x 58
D.M.C. COLOR CODE

.	Unstitched	
z	Yellow	726
o	Orange	970
x	Gold	972
●	Toast	434
v	Green	368

Star Flower is quilted using
8 diamond shaped pieced together. Sometimes called
Log Cabin Star.

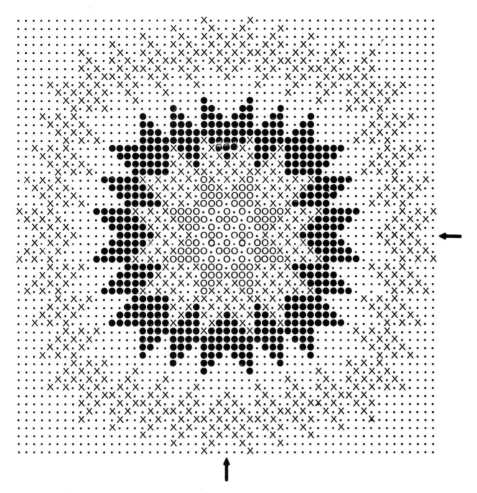

STAR OF THE EAST

STAR OF BETHLEHEM

SIZE - 55 x 55
D.M.C. COLOR CODE

.	Unstitched	
●	Blue	336
o	Wine	915
x	Pink	603

Some of the most beautiful
museum quilts are made from
this type of star pattern.
Each shape of this design is
over 5 stitches - only the
pattern changes. It is not
difficult to stitch.
Refer to Projects, Part III.

54

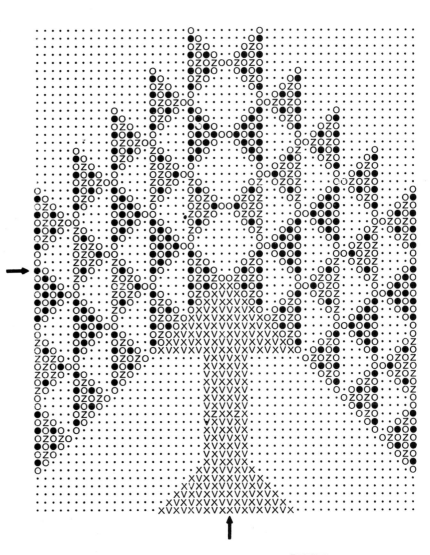

TREE OF LIFE

```
SIZE - 50 x 61
D.M.C. COLOR CODE

.    Unstitched
z    Light Green 704
o    Green       700
●    Red         349
x    Brown       801
v    Rust        301
```

There are many tree patterns among old quilts. You could call this Apple Tree, or Lemon Tree, if stitched with yellow. Refer to Projects, Part III.

55

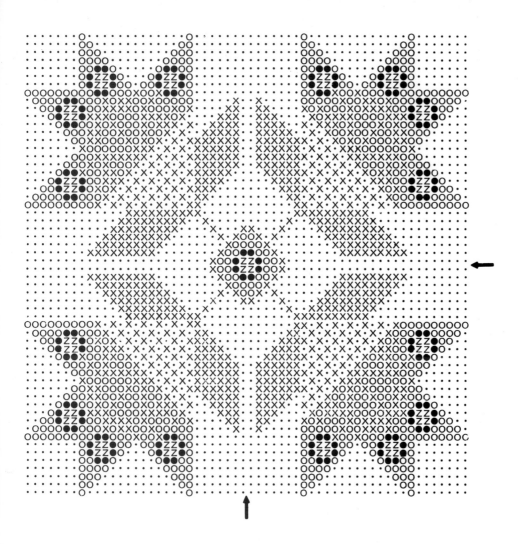

TULIPS

SIZE - 58 x 58
D.M.C. COLOR CODE

.	Unstitched	
●	Rust	919
x	Olive	3346
z	Yellow	972
o	Yellow	726

Flowers held an important place in the lives of pioneer women. There are a great many quilt patterns bearing the names of flowers.
Refer to Projects, Part III.

56

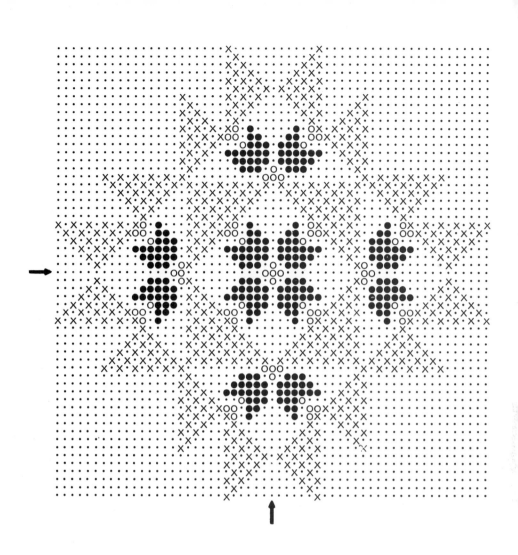

UNION SQUARE

SIZE - 57 x 57
D.M.C. COLOR CODE

.   Unstitched
●   Blue   517
o   Magenta718
x   Olive 937

Union Square is an old pattern
usually quilted in red, white,
and blue.   An easy pattern to
stitch, and a lovely design
grouped in fours.
Refer to Projects, Part III.

57

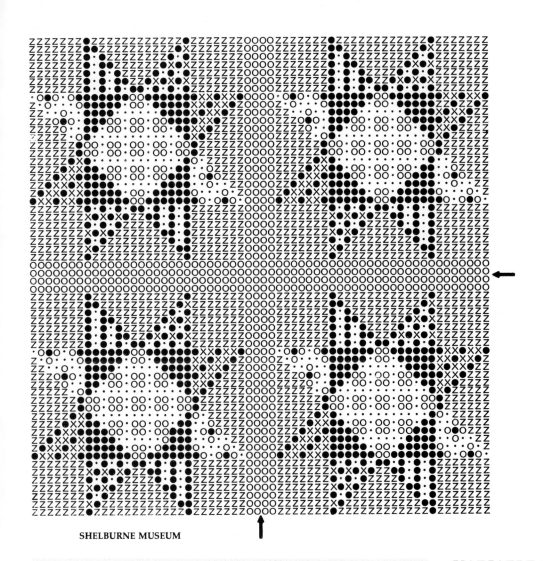

VARIABLE STAR

SIZE - 60 x 60
D.M.C. COLOR CODE

Star 1			Star 2		
.	Unstitched		.	Unstitched	
●	Red	498	●	Dk. Blue	796
z	Pink	605	z	Lt. Blue	800
o	Blue	798	o	Green	912
x	Pink	603	x	Blue	798
v	Lilac	208	v	Purple	208

Star 3			Star 4		
.	Unstitched		.	Unstitched	
●	Green	699	●	Purple	550
z	Green	955	z	Lilac	210
o	Purple	208	o	Magenta	718
x	Green	912	x	Lilac	208
v	Blue	798	v	Blue	798

This pattern is actually 4 blocks together. The o symbol for the inside border is Blue 797.

58

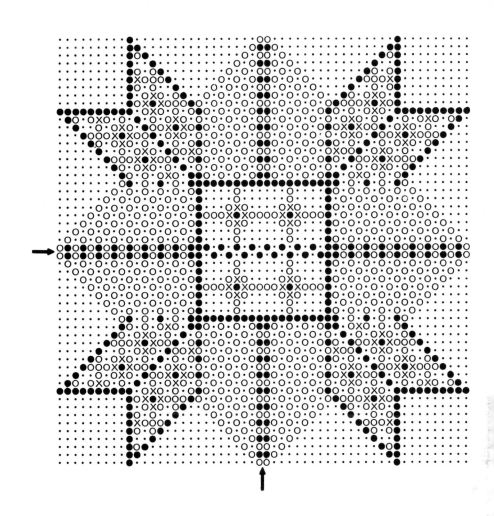

WEATHER VANE

SIZE - 56 x 56
D.M.C. COLOR CODE

```
.   Unstitched
●   Dark Brown  801
o   Med. Brown  434
x   Gold        725
```

This is an old pattern
from the days when almost
everyone had a weather vane
on the barn roof.

59

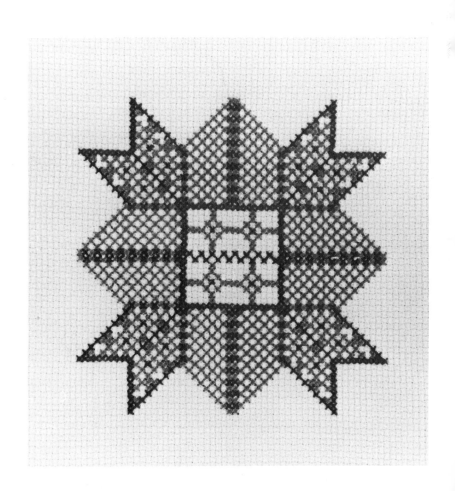

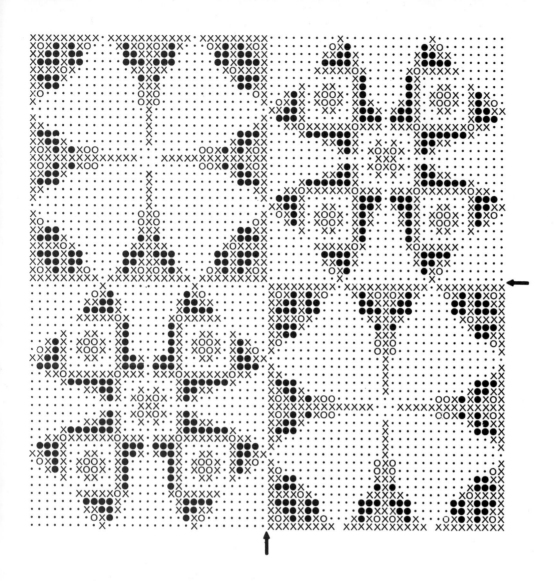

WHEEL OF MYSTERY

SIZE - 62 x 62
D.M.C. COLOR CODE

.	Unstitched	
x	Gold	781
●	Red	817
o	Olive	3346

One side of this block will fit
exactly into the other and form
a square. This concept has been
used in many quilt patterns.

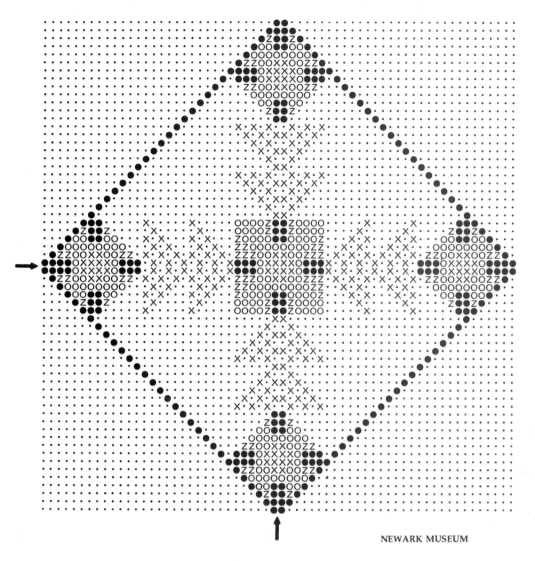

WILD GOOSE CHASE

SIZE - 62 x 62
D.M.C. COLOR CODE

.	Unstitched	
o	Bittersweet	350
x	Coral	352
●	Rust	221
z	Lt. Coral	353

In patchwork design, triangle
shapes are characteristic of
bird symbols. See Winged Square
and Hovering Hawks.
Refer to Projects, Part III.

61

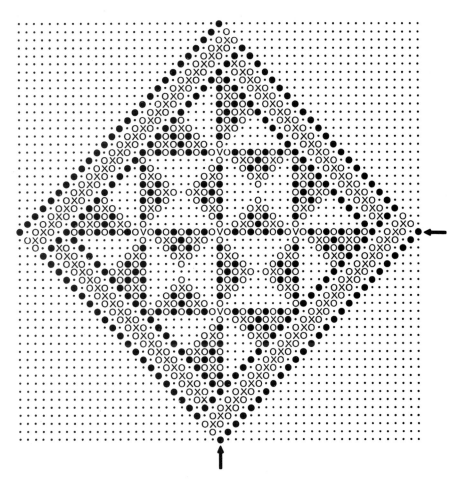

NEWARK MUSEUM

WINDMILL

BROKEN DISHES

```
SIZE - 53 x 53
D.M.C. COLOR CODE

.   Unstitched
v   Bittersweet  350
o   Lt. Coral    353
●   Med. Coral   352
x   Green        501
```

Triangle shapes are relatively
easy to work in counted cross-
stitch, and offer an endless
variety of choices in design.
Refer to Projects, Part III.

62

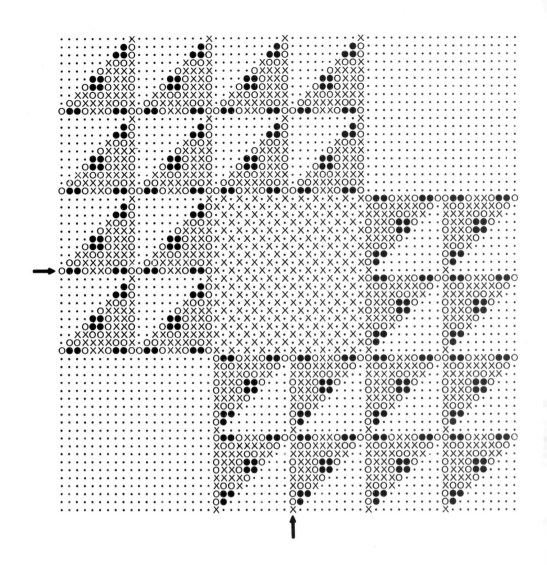

WINGED SQUARE

SIZE - 59 x 59
D.M.C. COLOR CODE

.   Unstitched
x   Blue   796
●   Red   321
o   Lt. Blue 799

Winged Square looks like a
flock of birds in flight.
It's a guess that that's
where the name came from.
Refer to Projects, Part III.

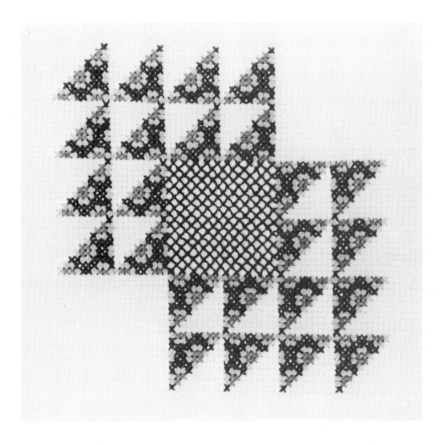

COLOR SECTION

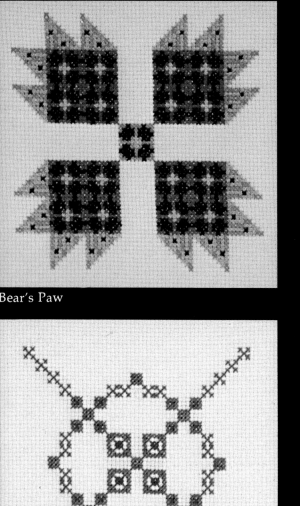

Bear's Paw

Cross and Crown

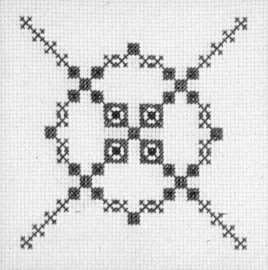

Burgoyne Surrounded

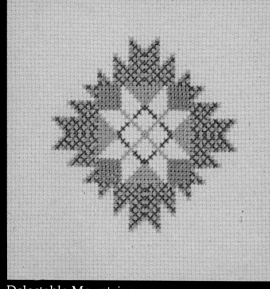

Delectable Mountains

Compass

Double Pinwheel

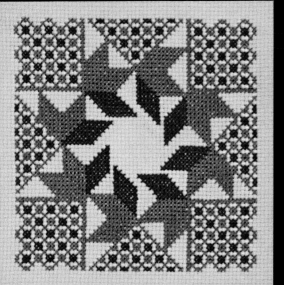

Falling Star

Goose in the Pond

Feathered Star

Hands all Around

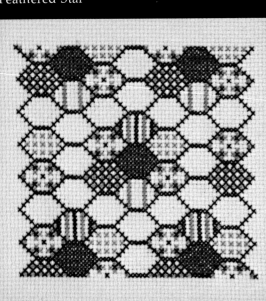

Flower Garden

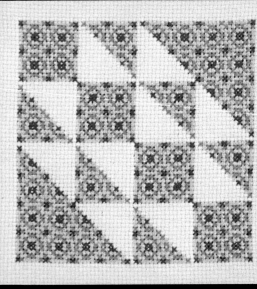

Hovering Hawks

Jack-in-the-Box

Lady of the Lake

Jackson Star

Lazy Daisy

Kaleidoscope

Lone Star

All of these projects have been stitched using the single-block designs as a base. Starting from the upper left-hand corner are: Eight-Pointed Star, with a circle of stars around it, stitched on off-white Aida cloth; Jackson Square stitched on off-white Aida cloth; a single Eight-Pointed Star with border stitched on beige Klosters; Yellow Tulips stitched on off-white Aida cloth; Lazy Daisy stitched on off-white Aida cloth; Cactus Rose stitched on pink Aida cloth; Tulips stitched on off-white Aida cloth; Tree of Life stitched on off-white Aida cloth; Double Pinwheel stitched on off-white Aida cloth; Pieced Star stitched on beige Floba; Wild Goose Chase stitched on off-white Aida cloth; and Burgoyne Surrounded stitched on off-white Aida cloth. Note the differences, both in design and fabric, between the three Eight-Pointed Stars, all of which can be achieved using a single Eight-Pointed Star block.

PART 3

THE PROJECTS

Use the block designs in Part 2 to make pillows, pictures, and more. The drawings in this section show how some of the block designs can be used alone or combined to form a design pattern for a project. Border or margin designs are included for many.

For example, the Pieced Star block from Part 2 has been grouped with three others of its kind to form a design. A border surrounds the entire design and helps to set it off. This would make a fine pillow top. On the same page the Pieced Star is shown singly with an interesting border design, which serves as a mat effect for a framed picture.

It is important to be able to figure out how many stitches there are in the total design so that you can purchase the right amount of fabric, and, knowing the stitch count, you can determine how large your finished piece will be. Again using the Pieced Star as an example, you'll notice that the size indicated is 153 × 153.

This means that the *stitched* area of the design is 153 stitches horizontally and 153 stitches vertically. (The first number on all projects is the count in a horizontal direction; the second number is the count in a vertical direction.) This particular project is equal in count horizontally and vertically; some are not.

This design incorporates four of the single Pieced Star blocks plus a border. Margins are *not* included in the count, so before purchasing your fabric, make sure you add enough fabric for a margin if you choose to have one. In all cases make sure you have enough fabric for a seam allowance. It's a good idea to double-check the count to make sure you understand before starting any project.

It would be a good idea here to review the way in which a stitched area is counted. Start with the last space on the left within the design area. In the case of Pieced Star this means the border. You can see by looking at the chart for the border that it is 9 stitches wide. Then look at the drawing for the entire design. The 3 represents 3 blank spaces before your first star begins. From the single block chart in Part II we know the star is 64 stitches. There is 1 space between the first star and the second star, and, of course, the second star is 64 stitches. There are 3 spaces between the second star and the beginning of the right side border, and the right border is 9 stitches wide. Now check the count in a vertical direction the same way. Use

a pencil and paper and add it all up:

9	Left Border
3	Blank Spaces
64	First Star
1	Blank Space
64	Second Star
3	Blank Spaces
9	Right Border
153	Total stitches in design area

An indication is given on each project as to the best place to start to stitch. Providing your stitch count is correct and you have started at the suggested place, your borders will fall right into place.

Before purchasing your fabric, be sure you know exactly how much you need. Again, using the Pieced Star as an example, with #14 Aida cloth, these 153 stitches × 153 stitches should finish very close to 11 inches (28 × 28 cm.). (Remember, to figure this out for yourself simply divide the count of your cloth into the count of your stitches.) If you wanted to add a 1½-inch (4-cm.) margin on all sides, you could make a 14-inch (35½-cm.) finished pillow or framed picture.

So far, no allowance has been made for a seam allowance for finishing. For this it is safe to add another 2 inches (5 cm.) on all sides before purchasing your fabric. For the Pieced Star Pillow there are 11 inches (28 cm.) of design area, a 1½-inch (4-cm.) margin all around, and a 2-inch (5-cm.) seam allowance all around. All this adds up to an 18-inch (46-cm.) square of fabric. All of the project sizes in this book can be arrived at in the same way.

When looking at the project drawings, do not be confused by the shaded areas—cross hatched, speckled, black, white, etc. These are meant merely as an indication of pattern areas. Refer to the single-block design for actual stitching instructions and color codes.

Not all of the design blocks in Part II are represented in Part III. If you choose to work on a block that does not appear here, simply determine the size of the single block, decide whether you want to use one or a group of blocks together, and add up the stitches. Be sure to include spaces between blocks and add borders and margins, if you choose to have them.

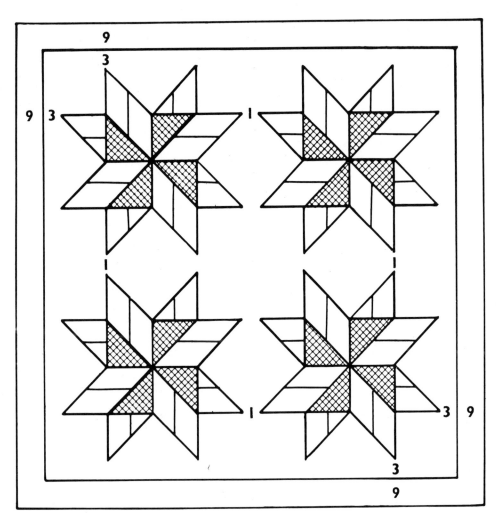

PIECED STAR A

SIZE - 153 x 153

This piece makes an attractive pillow top. Leave a margin on all 4 sides. Start at the border. See chart.

Stitched Area
#11 Aida: 14" x 14"
 (35½ cm. x 35½ cm.)
#14 Aida: 11" x 11"
 (28 cm. x 28 cm.)

Border

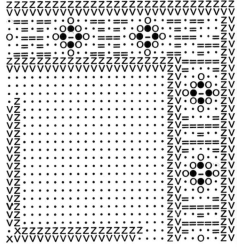

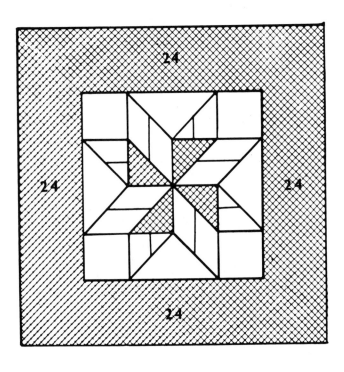

PIECED STAR B

SIZE - 112 x 112

This design works well as a framed picture. A 2" border stitched in the cross hatch pattern serves as a mat when framed. Start from the center.

Stitched Area
#11 Aida: 10" x 10"
 (25 cm. x 25 cm.)
#14 Aida: 8" x 8"
 (20 cm. x 20 cm.)

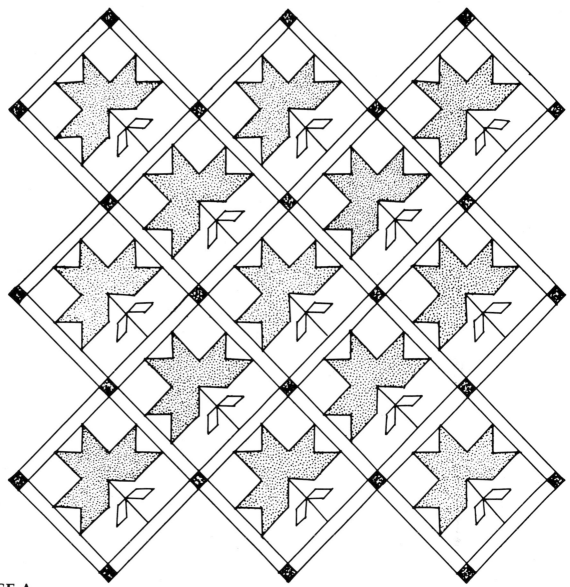

CACTUS ROSE A

SIZE - 139 x 139
This block is suitable for a pillow
top. Start stitching in the center.
Cactus Rose colors are pretty on
pink fabric.
     Stitched Area
#11 Aida: 11½'' x 11½''
     (29 cm. x 29 cm.)
#14 Aida: 10'' x 10''
     (25 cm. x 25 cm.)

JACKSON STAR A

SIZE - 68 x 68
This single-block design bordered by one
row of stitches looks well framed. Try
an initial in the center unstitched area.
     Stitched Area
#11 Aida: 6'' x 6''
     (15 cm. x 15 cm.)
#14 Aida: 5'' x 5''
     (13 cm. x 13 cm.)

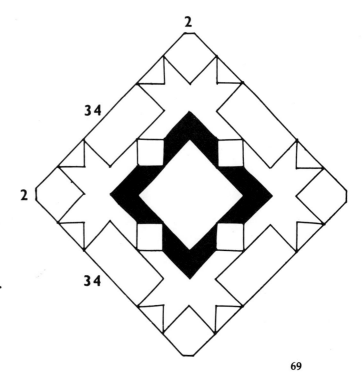

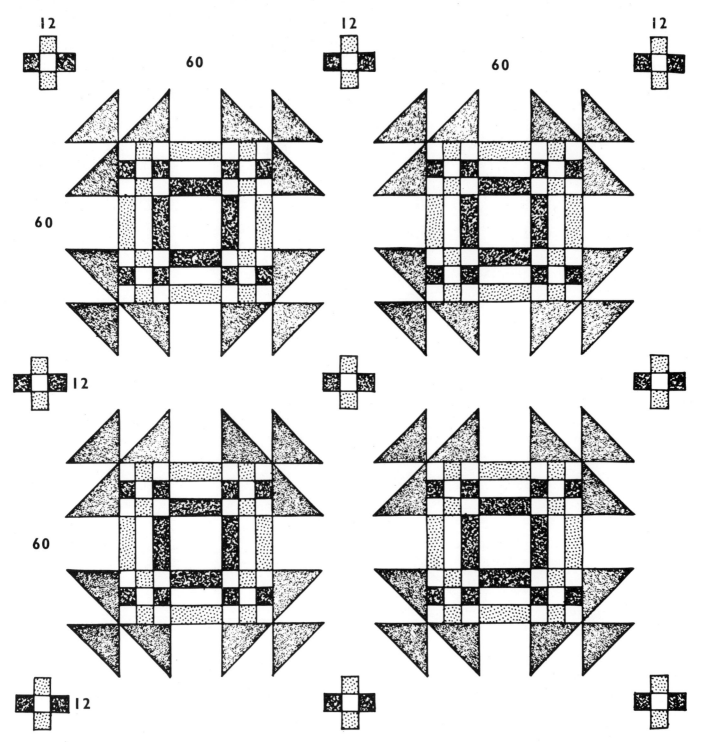

GOOSE IN THE POND

SIZE - 156 x 156

There is no border for this design. The
cross motif is set in space. See chart
for placement. Start stitching at upper
right-hand corner.

     Stitched Area

#11 Aida: 14'' x 14''

      (35½ cm. x 35½ cm.)

#14 Aida: 11'' x 11''

      (28 cm. x 28 cm.)

Cross Motif

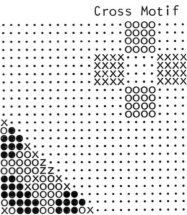

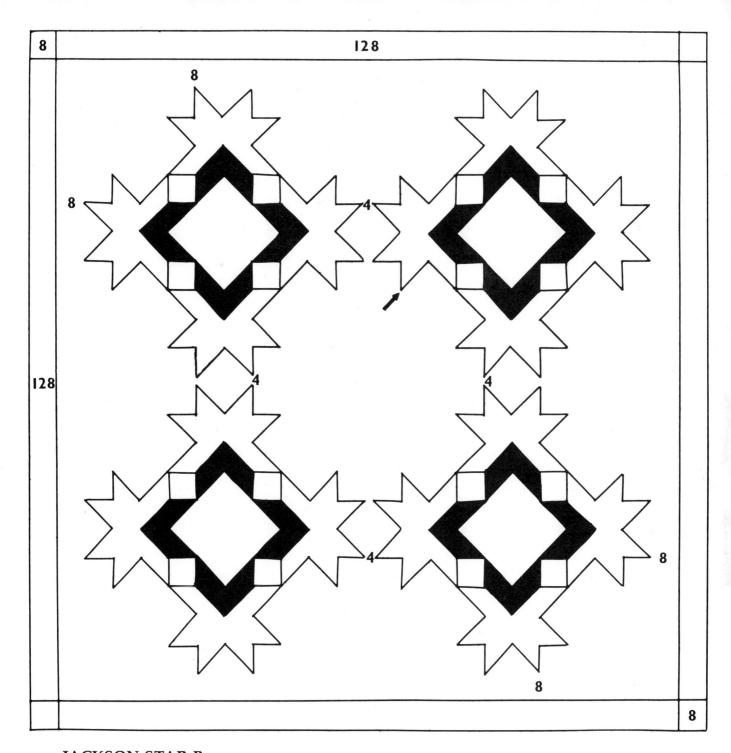

JACKSON STAR B

SIZE - 143 x 143

This design, 4 blocks together with a border and a margin, looks very well framed. Start stitching 2 spaces up and 24 spaces to the right of the center of your fabric. See arrow.

    Stitched Area
#11 Aida: 13" x 13"
    (33 cm. x 33 cm.)
#14 Aida: 10" x 10"
    (25 cm. x 25 cm.)

Border

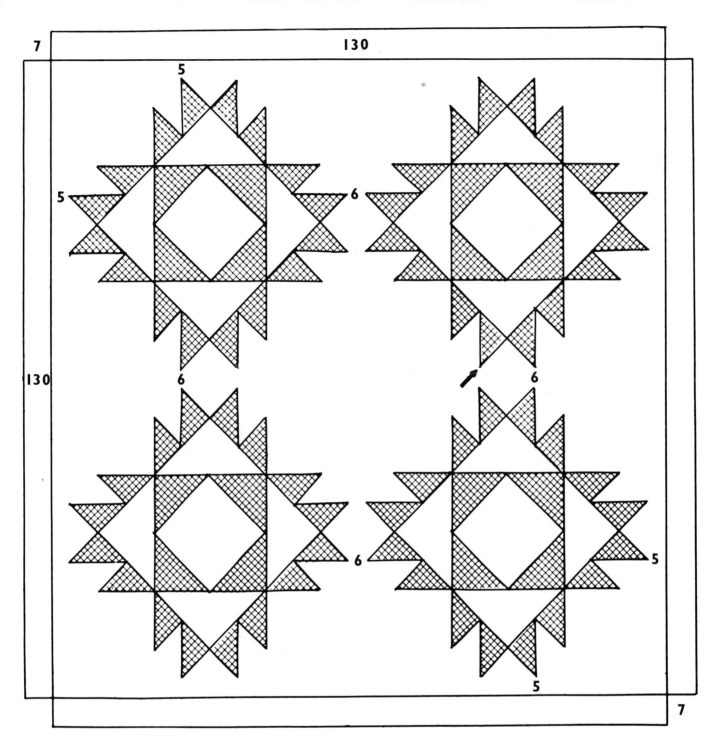

UNION SQUARE A

SIZE - 144 x 144

Start from the center of your
fabric, 3 spaces up and 25 spaces
to the right. See arrow. You
can also start at the border as
shown on the chart.

Stitched Area
#11 Aida: 13" x 13"
    (33 cm. x 33 cm.)
#14 Aida: 10" x 10"
    (25 cm. x 25 cm.)

Border

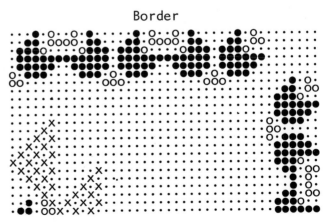

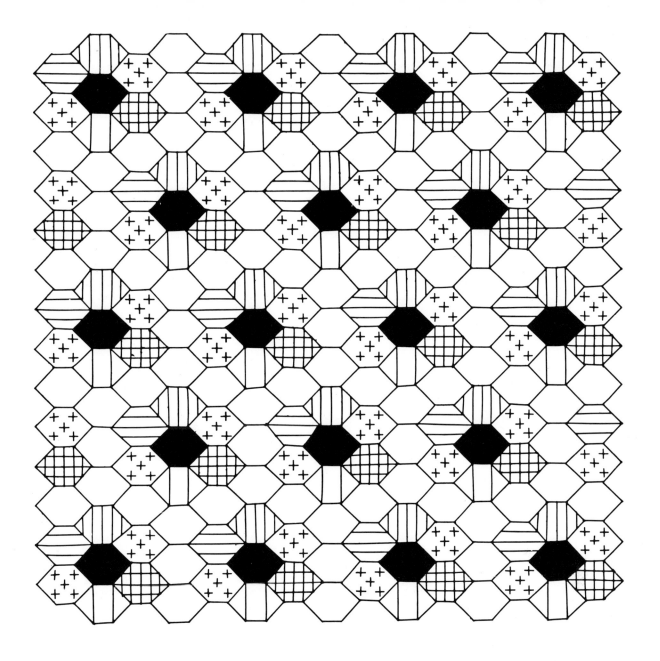

FLOWER GARDEN A

SIZE - 125 x 120

With an overall design of this nature, you can make almost any size you choose.

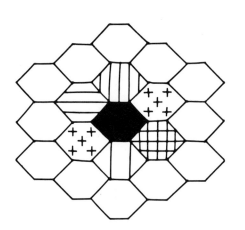

FLOWER GARDEN B

SIZE - 45 x 41

A single flower with one row of solid color around it is ideal for a small box. Start in the center.

MONKEY WRENCH

SIZE - 120 x 115

The unstitched squares on this project can be
stitched in cross hatch. Refer to the single
block design and you can see this more easily.
A pillow top is a good application for this
design.
    Stitched Area
#11 Aida: 11'' x 10½''
      (28 cm. x 27 cm.)
#14 Aida: 8½'' x 8''
      (21 cm. x 20 cm.)

LAZY DAISY

SIZE - 104 x 104

This project is made up of 4 block designs together, 2 across and 2 down. It has the effect of trellis work.

      Stitched Area

#11 Aida: $9\frac{1}{2}$'' x $9\frac{1}{2}$''
     (24 cm. x 24 cm.)

#14 Aida: $7\frac{1}{2}$'' x $7\frac{1}{2}$''
     (19 cm. x 19 cm.)

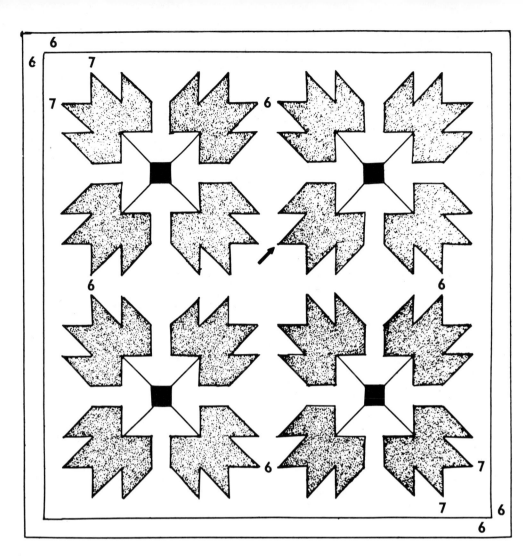

AUTUMN LEAVES A

SIZE - 156 x 156

Start stitching at the upper right-hand border as shown on the chart, or 3 spaces to the right and 13 spaces up from the center of your fabric. See arrow.

Stitched Area

#11 Aida: 14'' x 14''
(35½ cm. x 35½ cm.)

#14 Aida: 11'' x 11''
(28 cm. x 28 cm.)

Border for A

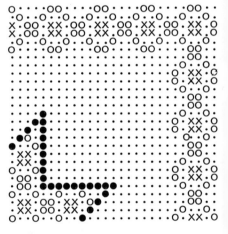

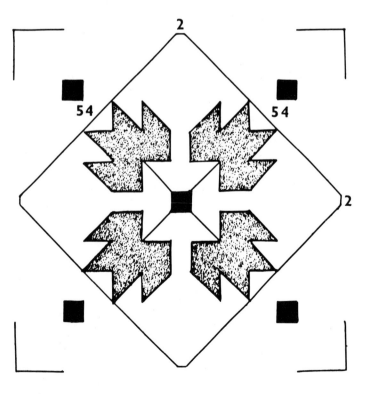

AUTUMN LEAVES B

SIZE - 108 x 108

One-block design bordered with a single line of stitches. Outside the border, the 4 black squares are the same as the stitched shape that is in the center of the block. This is good for framing.

Stitched Area

#11 Aida: 10'' x 10''
(25 cm. x 25 dm.)

#14 Aida; 8'' x 8''
(20 cm. x 20 cm.)

76

BLAZING STAR

SIZE - 141 x 141

An ambitious project to accomplish. Start at the
center with a single-block design. Continue to add
on the shapes, alternating the patterns of the original
block, according to the shading of this drawing -
all cross hatch one color, all dots another color, etc.
The shading represents the colors of the Blazing Star
block.

Stitched Area
#11 Aida: 13'' x 13''
     (33 cm. x 33 cm.)
#14 Aida: 10'' x 10''
     (25 cm. x 25 cm.)

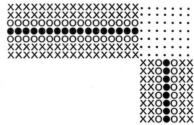

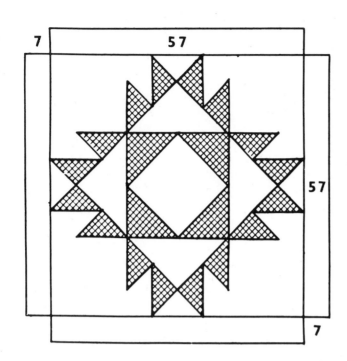

Double Pinwheel Border

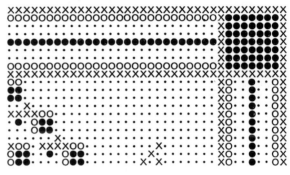

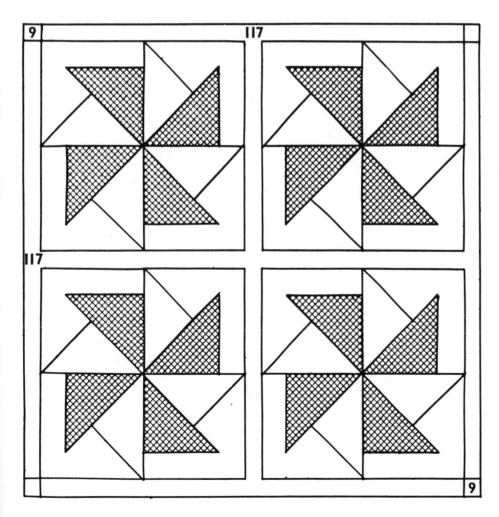

UNION SQUARE B

SIZE - 71 x 71

One block using a striped border.
     Stitched Area
#11 Aida: 6½'' x 6½''
     (17 cm. x 17 cm.)
#14 Aida: 5'' x 5''
     (13 cm. x 13 cm.)

DOUBLE PINWHEEL

SIZE - 135 x 135

Four blocks separated by the same patterned border, as shown on the chart.
     Stitched Area
#11 Aida: 12'' x 12''
     (30 cm. x 30 cm.)
#14 Aida: 9½'' x 9½''
     (24 cm. x 24 cm.)

WINDMILL

SIZE - 145 x 145

If you start the project at the upper right-hand corner, as the chart shows, this will be easy to follow. However, you can start at the center.
     Stitched Area
#11 Aida: 13'' x 13''
     (33 cm. x 33 cm.)
#14 Aida: 10'' x 10''
     (25 cm. x 25 cm.)

Border

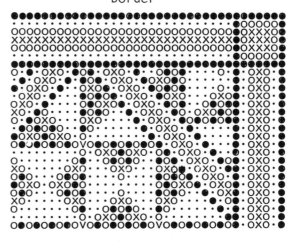

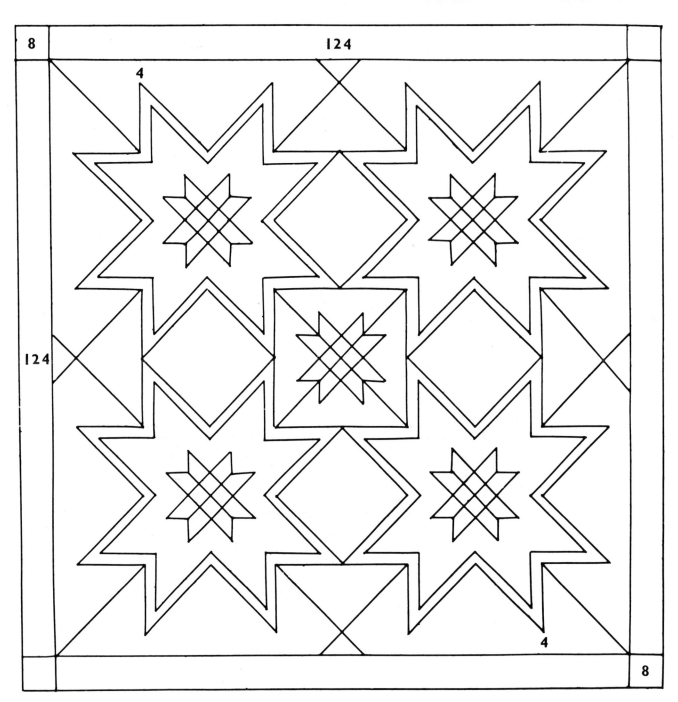

EIGHT-POINTED STAR A

SIZE - 140 x 140

A and B on these pages show two
ways of using the same block design. The crisscross background
is a single line of stitches. The
star at center is the same as the
center star of the block design.
Start at the border, or at center.

Stitched Area
#11 Aida: 12½'' x 12½''
    (32 cm. x 32 cm.)
#14 Aida: 10'' x 10''
    (25 cm. x 25 cm.)

BORDER

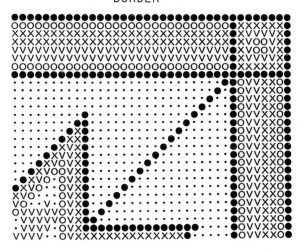

EIGHT-POINTED STAR B

SIZE - 120 x 120

This design has no border. It is placed centered on the
fabric with as much margin as you choose. The medium-
size stars are the same as the center star of the block.
The numbers between stars indicate count of unstitched
spaces between stars. The point of one star is on the
same line as the point of the next star. Start at the
center.

    Stitched Area
#11 Aida: 11'' x 11''
    (28 cm. x 28 cm.)
#14 Aida: 8½'' x 8½''
    (21½ cm. x 21½ cm.)

STAR OF THE EAST

SIZE - 87 x 87

This is a single-block design with only the points
added to form a star. All the shapes that are shaded
alike should be colored the same. The stars in the
corners are identical to the center star of the block.

    Stitched Area
#11 Aida: 8'' x 8''
    (20 cm. x 20 cm.)
#14 Aida: 6'' x 6''
    (15 cm. x 15 cm.)

82

DELECTABLE MOUNTAINS

SIZE - 120 x 120

This design can become as large as you choose, simply by
adding more rows of mountains. The center is a single
block, and the mountains surround it.
     Stitched Area
#11 Aida: 11'' x 11''
     (28 cm. x 28 cm.)
#14 Aida: 8½'' x 8½''
     (21½ cm. x 21½ cm.)

BURGOYNE SURROUNDED

SIZE - 165 x 165

These 9 blocks make a very
pretty patch pillow. Start
stitching in the center.
    Stitched Area
#11 Aida: 15" x 15"
    (38 cm. x 38 cm.)
#14 Aida: 12" x 12"
    (30 cm. x 30 cm.)

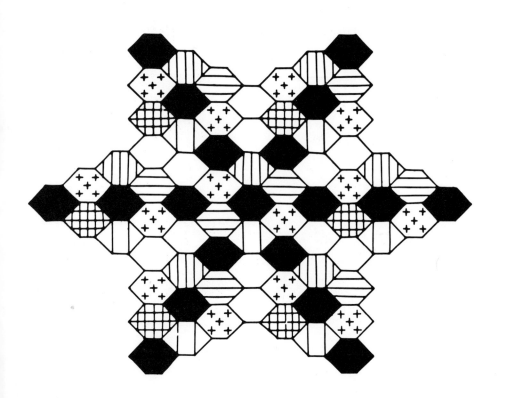

FLOWER GARDEN C

SIZE - 110 x 81

The hexagon shapes are
put together to form a
star shape. Start to
stitch at the center of
this design.
    Stitched Area
#11 Aida: 10" x 7¼"
    (25 cm. x 18 cm.)
#14 Aida: 8" x 6"
    (20 cm. x 15 cm.)

TREE OF LIFE

SIZE - 102 x 102

A single line of stitches borders this block. It is suitable for a pillow or a framed picture.

Stitched Area
#11 Aida: 9" x 9"
   (23 cm. x 23 cm.)
#14 Aida: 7" x 7"
   (18 cm. x 18 cm.)

MY MOTHER'S STAR

SIZE - 100 x 100

Many designs can be put together in this way. The background is single line stitches, crisscrossed, which, when finished, look very much like quilting.

Stitched Area
#11 Aida: 9' x 9"
   (23 cm. x 23 cm.)
#14 Aida: 7" x 7"
   (18 cm. x 18 cm.)

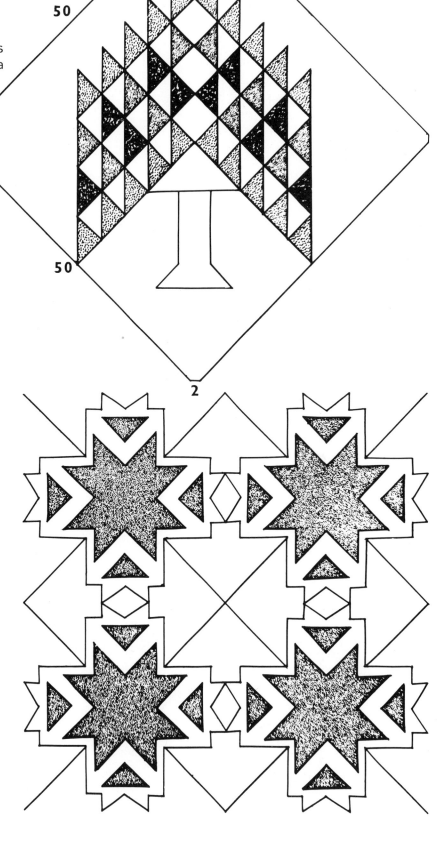

WILD GOOSE CHASE A

SIZE - 132 x 108

The border is made up of the same shapes
and pattern as the blocks. If a margin
is left only at top and bottom of
this project, it works well. Start
stitching at the center.
Stitched Area
#11 Aida: 12" x 10"
(30 cm. x 25 cm.)
#14 Aida: 9½" x 8"
(24 cm. x 20 cm.)

WILD GOOSE CHASE B

SIZE - 124 x 124

Put together in this way
each block fits into the other.
Begin at the center.
Stitched Area
#11 Aida: 10½ x 10½"
(27 cm. x 27 cm.)
#14 Aida: 9" x 9"
(23 cm. x 23 cm.)

WINGED SQUARE A

SIZE - 170 x 170

The triangular border reverses itself at the center of each side of the border. The square at each center is 10 spaces. Start to stitch, as the chart shows, at the upper left-hand corner, or find the center of the fabric; move 5 spaces up and 15 spaces to the left. See arrow.
  Stitched Area
#11 Aida: 15½'' x 15½''
     (39 cm. x 39 cm.)
#14 Aida: 12'' x 12''
     (30½ cm. x 30½ cm.)

Border for A

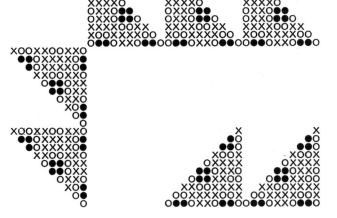

WINGED SQUARE B

SIZE - 120 x 120

The same block design, 4 together, but pointing in different directions. Leave the large square in the center unstitched, or fill it in with the cross hatch pattern.
  Stitched Area
#11 Aida: 11'' x 11''
     (28 cm. x 28 cm.)
#14 Aida: 8½'' x 8½''
     (22 cm. x 22 cm.)

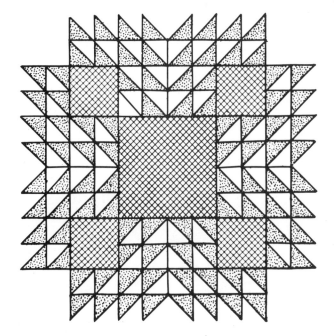

CHRISTMAS STAR A

SIZE - 135 x 135

This project is meant to be stitched without a border. It is an extension of the single block, with longer arms and an alternating pattern. The stars at each end are the same as the center.

Stitched Area
#11 Aida: 11'' x 11''
    (28 cm. x 28 cm.)
#14 Aida: 9½'' x 9½''
    (24 cm. x 24 cm.)

CHRISTMAS STAR B

SIZE - 37 x 37

This is the center star plus one motif. It is a good size for coasters or a keepsake box top.

Stitched Area
#11 Aida: 3½'' x 3¼'
    (9 cm. x 9 cm.)
#14 Aida: 2½'' x 2½''
    (6 cm. x 6 cm.)

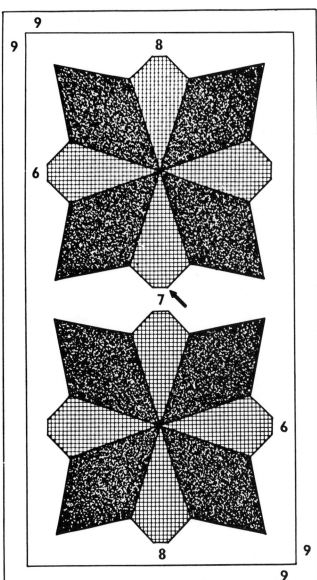

PINCUSHION

SIZE - 53 x 37

Try this design for a playing
card box. Start at the center.
     Stitched Area
#11 Aida: 5" x 3¼"
     (12 cm. x 8 cm.)
#14 Aida: 4" x 2½"
     (10 cm. x 6 cm.)

COMPASS

SIZE - 89 x 159

This is a good size for a serving
tray or it can be framed. The
chart shows the placement of the
Compass block in relationship to
the flower border. Start at the
upper right corner of border or
from the center of fabric, 3 spaces
up and 3 spaces to the right. See
arrow.
     Stitched Area
#11 Aida: 8" x 14½"
     (20 cm. x 37 cm.)
#14 Aida: 6½" x 11½"
     (16 cm. x 29 cm.)

Border

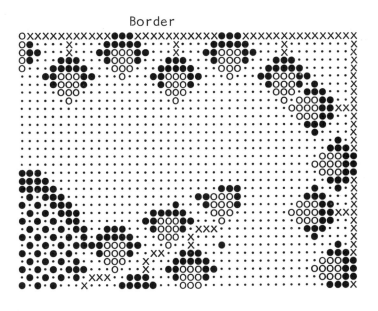

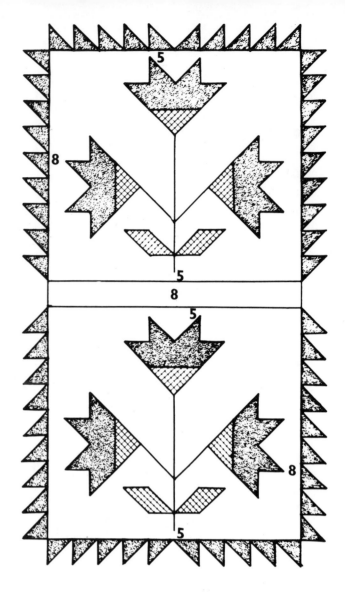

TULIPS

SIZE - 94 x 206

This is a good size for a breakfast tray. Start at upper right-hand corner of the border, as shown on the chart, or start at the center of the project.

    Stitched Area
#11 Aida: 8½'' x 19''
    (21½ cm. x 48 cm.)
#14 Aida: 7'' x 15''
    (18 cm. x 38 cm.)

90

NORTH CAROLINA LILY

SIZE - 96 x 168

Start at the upper right-hand corner of the border, as shown on the chart. Use the same pattern as leaves for the white divider between flowers.
    Stitched Area
#11 Aida: 9'' x 15''
    (23 cm. x 38 cm.)
#14 Aida: 7'' x 12''
    (17 cm. x 30 cm.)

Border for Tulips

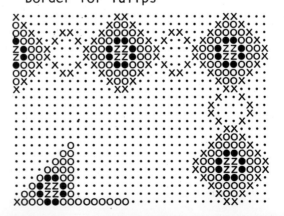

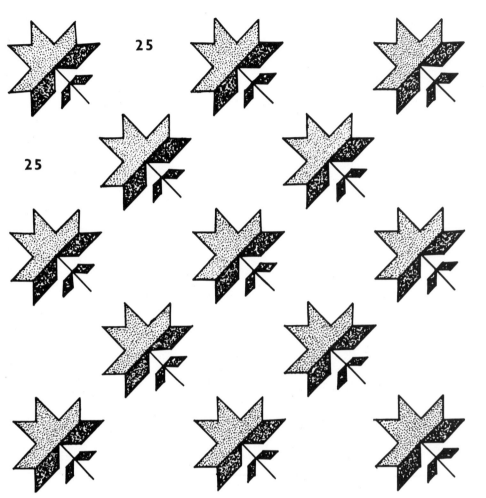

25

25

CACTUS ROSE B

SIZE - 51 x 51

This single design is good for a keepsake box or coasters.

    Stitched Area
#11 Aida: 5" x 5"
    (13 cm. x 13 cm.)
#14 Aida: 3½" x 3½"
    (9 cm. x 9 cm.)

North Carolina Lily Border
(See opposite page)

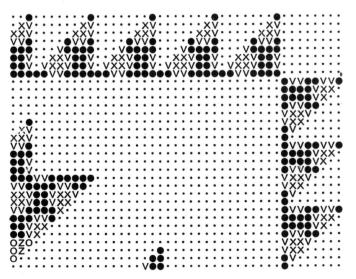

CACTUS ROSE C

SIZE - 125 x 125

These flowers are 25 spaces away from each other, and each flower is 25 spaces. Start your stitching with the center flower. Try using one of the small patterns from the pattern pages for the flower, and solid dark green for the stems and leaves.

    Stitched Area
#11 Aida: 11" x 11"
    (28 cm. x 28 cm.)
#14 Aida: 9" x 9"
    (23 cm. x 23 cm.)

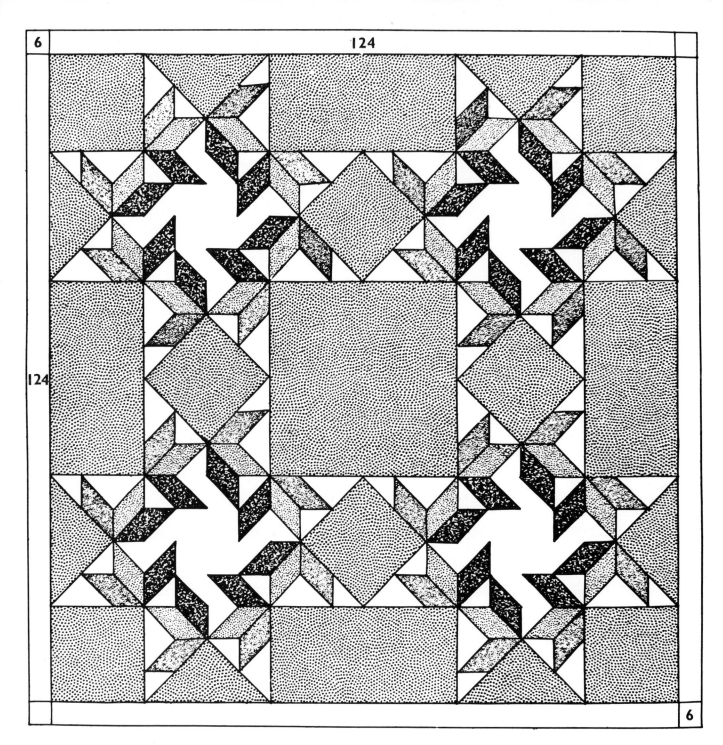

FALLING STAR

SIZE - 136 x 136

This pattern makes an attractive
pillow. Start at the upper right-
hand corner of the border, as chart
shows, or at the center.
     Stitched Area
#11 Aida: 13½'' x 13½''
    (34 cm. x 34 cm.)
#14 Aida: 9½'' x 9½''
    (24 cm. x 24 cm.)

Border

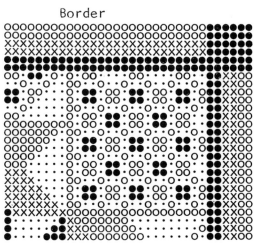

PART 4

THE PATTERNS WITHIN THE BLOCKS

On the following pages you will find the patterns I have used within the block designs in Part II. They are named according to the block design from which they were taken, and my purpose in providing them here is to enable you to interchange block designs and patterns. For example, you might want to use the Winged Square block from Part II, but not the pattern within the block. You would rather use the diagonal stripe from the triangle shape of Variable Star or the checkerboard pattern from the hexagon shape of Mosaic Variation. The following instructions will show you how to accomplish this.

Think of each of these patterns as a piece of printed fabric. If you were to cut triangles out of this fabric for a quilt, the pattern would fall haphazardly. However, with counted cross-stitch, it is very easy to match pattern much as you would when sewing a pocket on a print dress or when matching the stripes of a collar on a shirt.

To change any pattern you will need the following materials:

A pad of graph paper: It doesn't matter what size graph, but I use 8-to-the-inch because it's easier to see.

A pencil and eraser.

Scissors: These are for cutting paper, not fabric.

An ordinary ruler

The page on Block Shapes in Part 5 (Figure 20) includes all the shapes found in the block designs. Study the page carefully. Take all separate shapes from the design you have chosen, and draw them, well spaced from each other and according to count, on a piece of graph paper. Draw them in the same kind of steps you see on the Block Shapes page. Let's say you have one square and as many triangles as in Winged Square. Draw one triangle (since they are all the same size and pattern) and the one square, well spaced from each other and according to their counts, as shown in Figures 6 and 7.

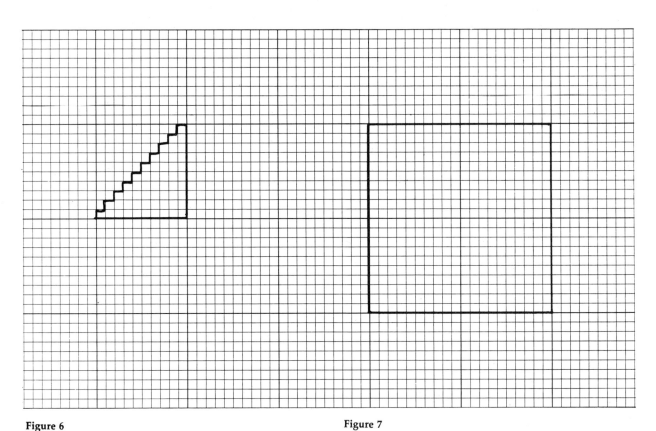

Figure 6

Triangle shape for Winged Square.

Figure 7

Square shape for Winged Square.

Next, draw the whole Winged Square design, in steps, on another clean piece of graph paper. This will really look like an outline of Winged Square without symbols. It should look the same as Figure 16 without the pattern added.

Go back to the original single triangle and square shape. Cut them out, leaving an ample margin, as shown in Figures 8 and 9. Then cut out the single shapes in steps. You have just made two paper templates. Now choose the patterns you prefer to use for these shapes from the pattern pages in this section. I chose the designs in Figures 10 and 11 for our example. Copy these patterns on the same size graph paper you used for your paper templates, as shown in Figures 12 and 13. Now lay your paper templates over one of the patterns and move it around until you find a balance that pleases you, as shown in Figures 14 and 15.

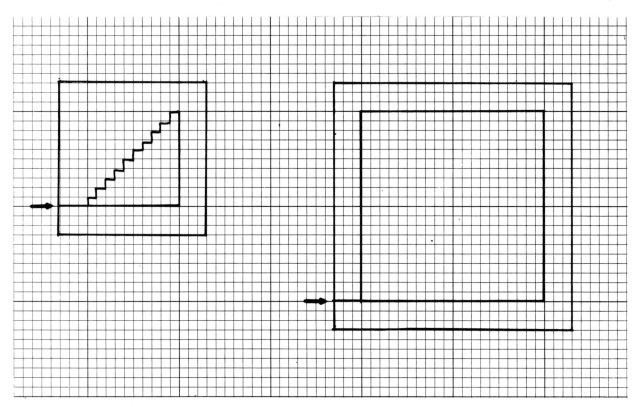

Figure 8

Cut from the arrow, along the triangle shape, including steps.

Figure 9

Cut from the arrow, around the square.

Figure 10

Pattern for the triangle shape of Winged Square from pattern pages.

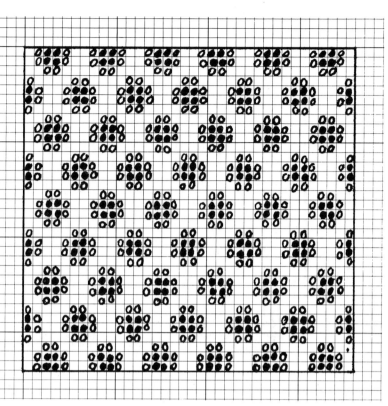

Figure 12

Pattern for the square shape copied on graph paper.

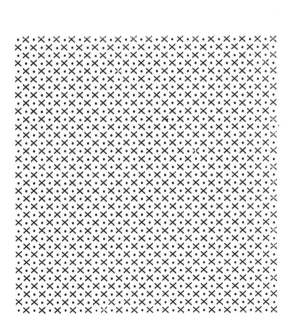

Figure 11

Pattern for the triangle shape copied on graph paper.

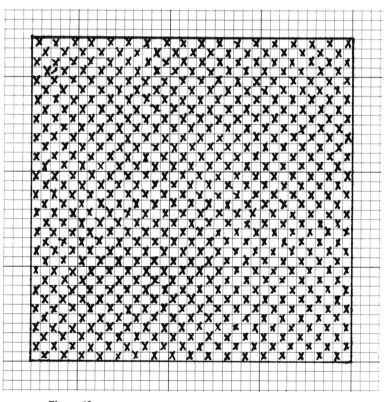

Figure 13

Pattern for the square shape of Winged Square from pattern pages.

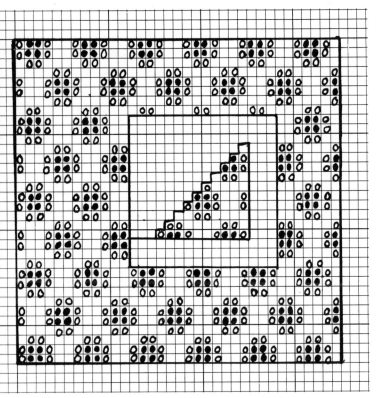

Figure 14
Triangle template placed over the pattern.

Figure 15
Square template placed over the pattern.

Pencil in all the symbols you see within the area of your templates on the outline you drew of Winged Square. In penciling in your symbols you need not put in the dot for a blank space. Since you are using graph paper, just leaving the space blank will be sufficient. See Figure 16.

If you discover you want the stitches of the triangle to be one color and the stitches of the square to be another, change one or the other to a different symbol. When your symbols are all finished on the whole block, all the ×'s should mean one color, all the ○'s another, and so on. This is how you color code.

If you decide to leave the ×'s on the triangle blank and to use the fabric itself as a color, your design will have an open, airy feeling. Pieced Star was finished in this way. If you choose to use the background as a color, but want the outline filled in, you can do that also. Hands All Around was done in this way. If it had not been, it would have had no form, and there would have been too much open work. Refer to insert for a quarter of the Winged Square block stitched in six different patterns. It will give you a good idea of the various ways pattern and color change these designs. You will see a small change in the way I stitched some of these. For Pieced Star pattern, upper left, I used only one vertical row of color, instead of two as the pattern shows. I did this for balance. For Winged Square pattern, lower right, I wanted the pattern to be open, so I left the background color dark blue. Then I added 1 stitch at the top of each triangle, in light blue, so that the triangles would meet and form a better visual triangle shape. So you see, these patterns can be adapted to your needs.

If you have fears about color and are insecure about starting to stitch, purchase a package of coloring pencils and color in your graph, square by square, before stitching the pattern. Use the color pencil closest to the thread color you want. (Do not color so heavily that your symbols are covered up.) This will give you a pretty good idea of how your finished piece will look. Still not sure? Stitch one shape on a piece of extra fabric in the exact colors you will be using.

Remember, if you are using 8-to-the-inch graph paper and want to stitch on #14 Aida, your stitched block will be much smaller than the graph paper block design. If you want to stitch on #11 Aida, your block will be smaller, but not much so.

Look at the Block Shapes page in Part 5, page 112. You will see that they are the shapes used to make up most of the block designs in Part 2. The shapes on page 112 may be smaller or larger than those used in the block designs, but they are the same shapes. You need only enlarge or reduce an individual shape to arrive at the size you choose to use. Always refer to the original block when only changing a pattern within the block, and use the shape exactly as in the original block.

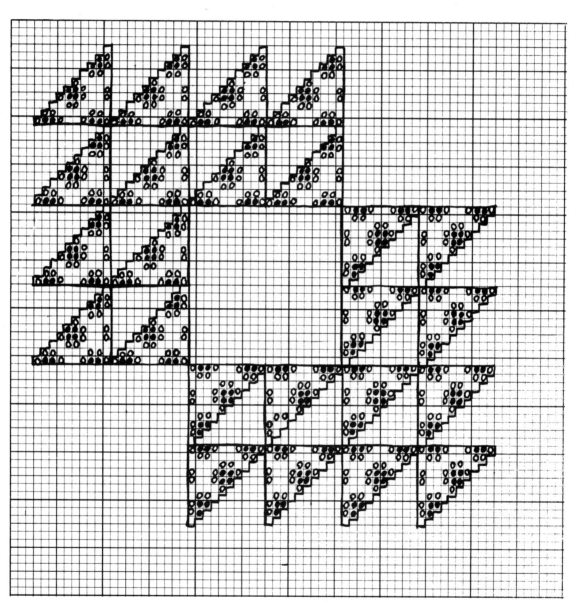

Figure 16
Completed design of Winged Square, using two patterns.

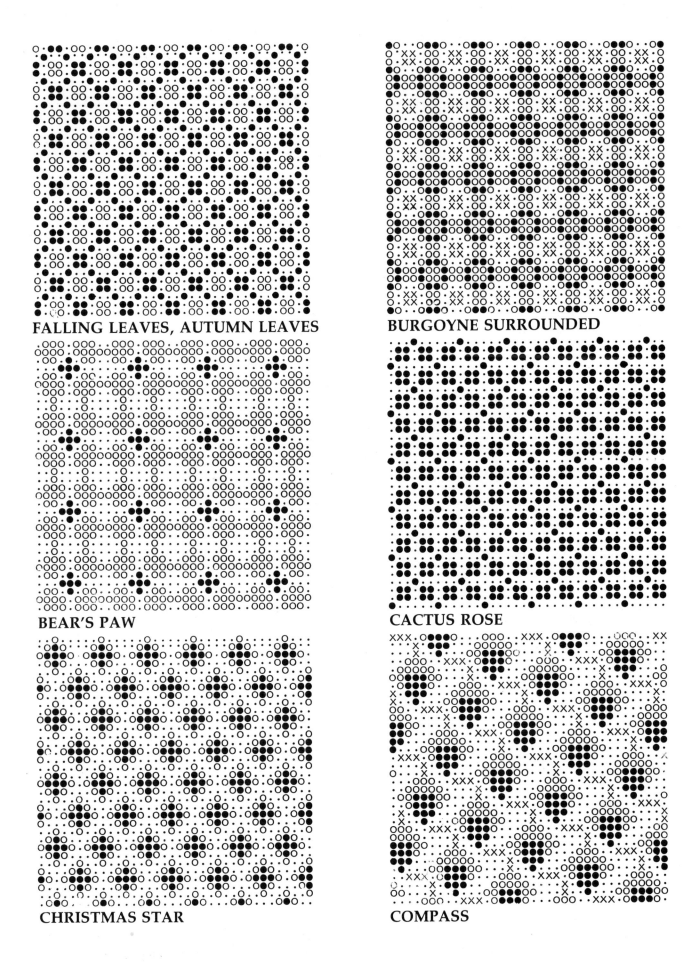

FALLING LEAVES, AUTUMN LEAVES

BURGOYNE SURROUNDED

BEAR'S PAW

CACTUS ROSE

CHRISTMAS STAR

COMPASS

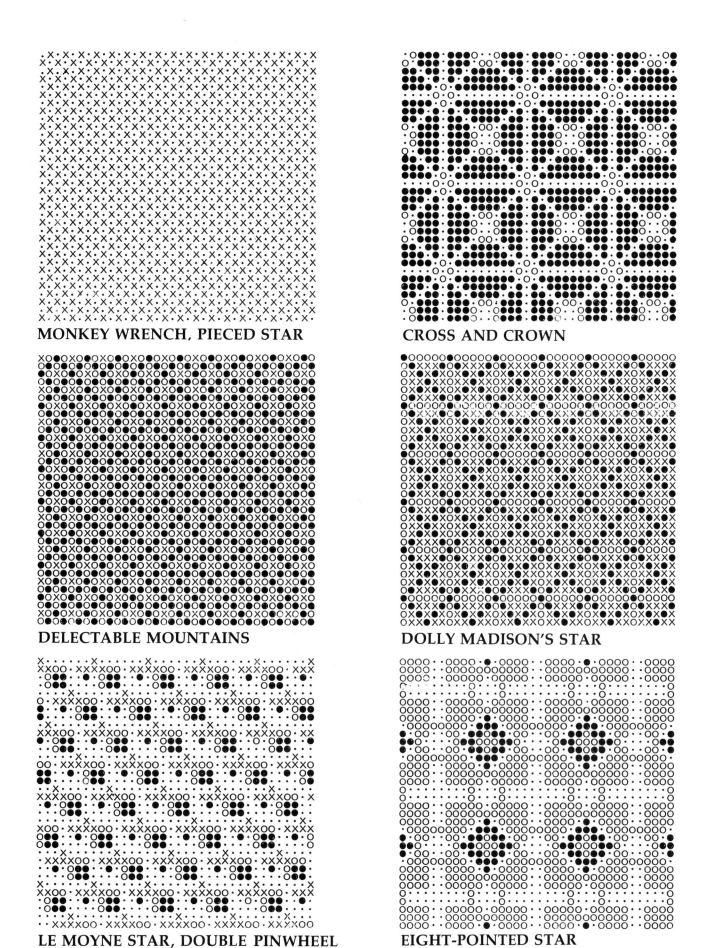

MONKEY WRENCH, PIECED STAR

CROSS AND CROWN

DELECTABLE MOUNTAINS

DOLLY MADISON'S STAR

LE MOYNE STAR, DOUBLE PINWHEEL

EIGHT-POINTED STAR

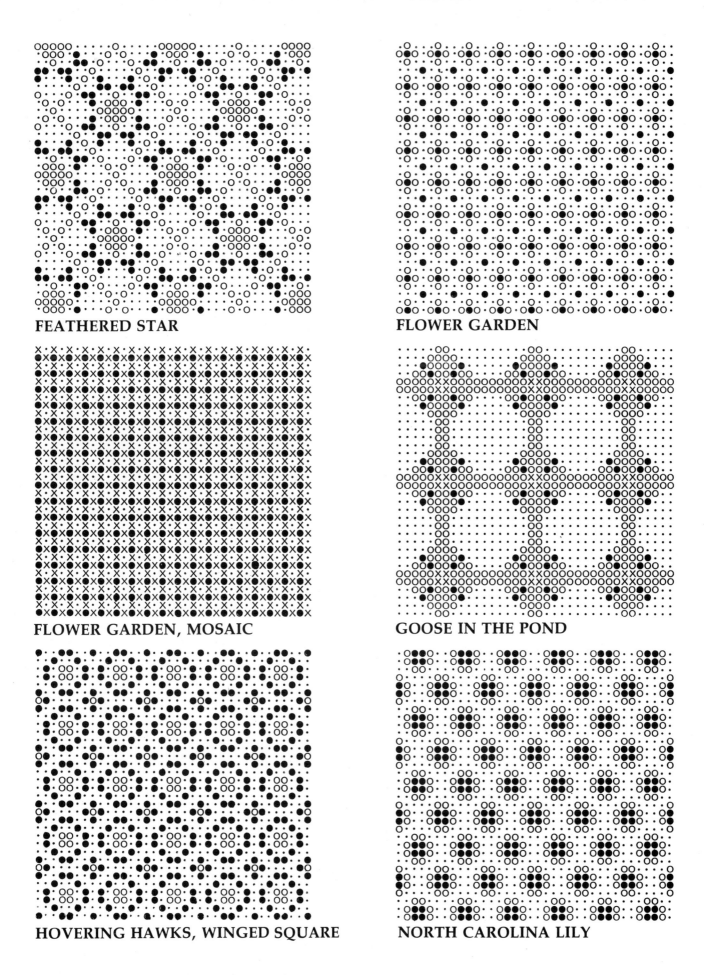

FEATHERED STAR

FLOWER GARDEN

FLOWER GARDEN, MOSAIC

GOOSE IN THE POND

HOVERING HAWKS, WINGED SQUARE

NORTH CAROLINA LILY

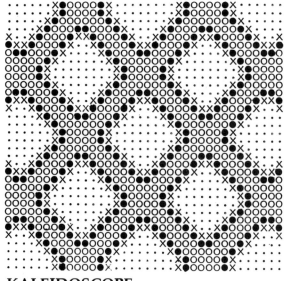

KALEIDOSCOPE

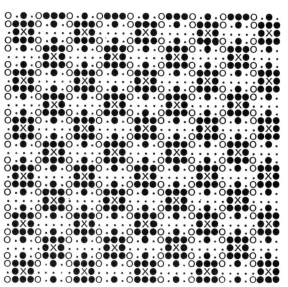

LADY OF THE LAKE

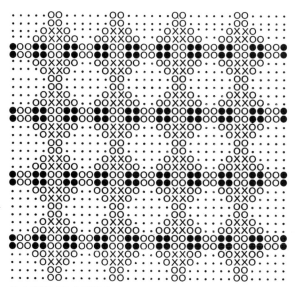

LAZY DAISY

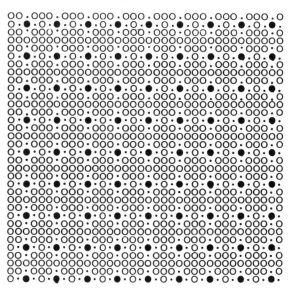

LONE STAR

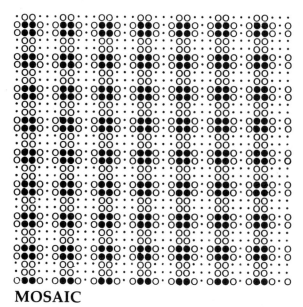

MOSAIC

MONKEY WRENCH

103

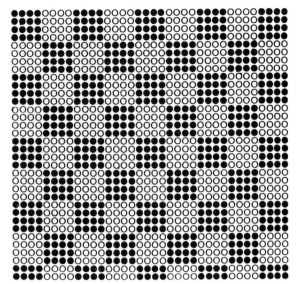

MOSAIC VARIATION

THREE-COLOR CHECKERBOARD

MRS. CLEVELAND'S CHOICE

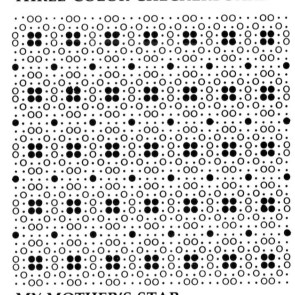

MY MOTHER'S STAR

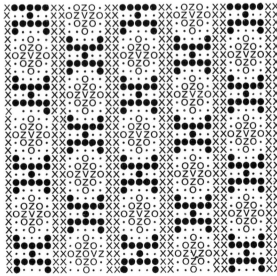

PIECED STAR

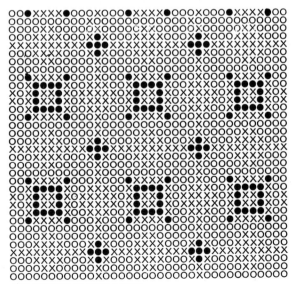

UNION SQUARE

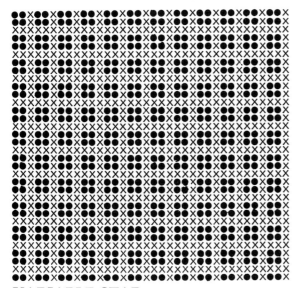

VARIABLE STAR

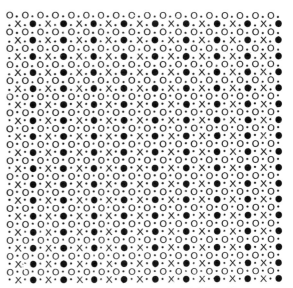

WINDMILL, BROKEN DISHES

WHEEL OF MYSTERY A

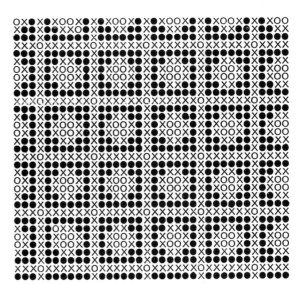

WHEEL OF MYSTERY B

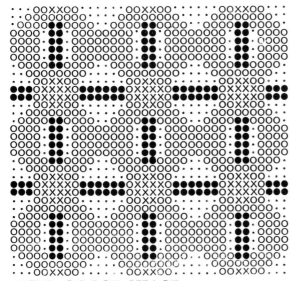

WILD GOOSE CHASE

EIGHT-POINTED STAR

VARIABLE STAR

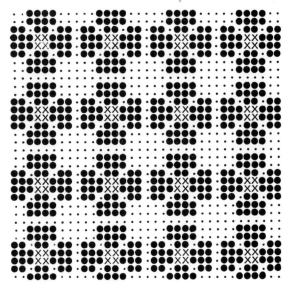

AUTUMN LEAVES

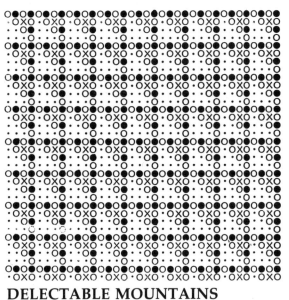

DELECTABLE MOUNTAINS

PINCUSHION

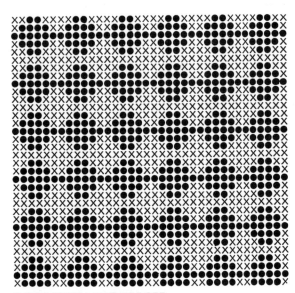

MONKEY WRENCH

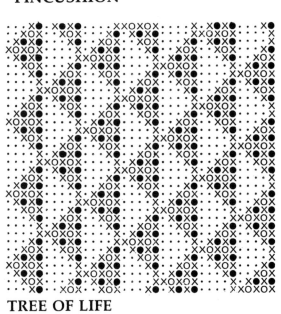

TREE OF LIFE

PART 5

THE DESIGNING OF
YOUR OWN WORK

Now that you are familiar with the basics you will no doubt want to do some designing on your own. The extra effort involved in designing your own work is well worth the time. You will be paid back handsomely, not only with an original design, but with a tremendous feeling of accomplishment, as well.

Do not labor over what you may think of as a big decision. Actually, you will be making many decisions as you go along, but each one is a small one. Taking your pencil in your hand to a piece of graph paper is the first major decision you will make. Avoid thinking about the entire project at once; you will be amazed at the number of design possibilities that occur to you.

One Step At a Time

The designing of your own piece should be approached in a step-by-step fashion as follows:

1. Decide the size you want your finished piece to be.
2. Choose the fabric you want—#14 Aida, #11 Aida, #22 Hardanger, etc.—and know it's stitch count.
3. Decide on the number of blocks—one, four, nine, etc.—you want in your design.
4. Decide whether you want borders and/or margins.
5. Decide on the size of your borders and/or margins.
6. Draw the simplest lines of your proposed project with a ruler. You have not determined the size of your block yet. That is automatically determined by all of the above.
7. Work out your single block according to the count of your line drawing.
8. Decide on pattern. Use one of the patterns given in Part 4 or work out your own.
9. Decide on colors.
10. Begin stitching.

Essentially, these steps fall into five categories—planning the overall project, planning the block, planning the pattern, planning the border (if one is used, that is), and planning color.

Planning the Project

Start out by knowing what you want to make—a pillow, framed picture, etc.—and how large it will be. Suppose that you want your finished piece to be 14 inches (35½ cm.)—a good size for a pillow. You know that you will be using #14 Aida cloth and you have a rough idea for a basic design. The design you have in mind consists of four blocks and you want a 2-inch (5-cm.) margin (in general, 1½- to 2-inch margins are a good size), but you are not sure yet if you want a border.

At this point you are ready to draw the simple lines of your design. Figures 17, 18, and 19 show three possibilities. In Figure 17 you have 2-inch (5-cm.) margins, leaving you four blocks at 5 inches (13 cm.) each. Multiply the size of your block—5—by the stitch count of your fabric—14—and you get the number of stitches in your block—70. Therefore, the size of your block is 70 × 70 stitches.

In Figure 18 you have drawn a 2½-inch margin and are leaving 1-inch (2½-cm.) spacing between blocks. The size of your block is 4 inches (10 cm.) square and, therefore, 56 × 56 stitches.

In Figure 19 you have decided that you might like a border. You still have 2-inch (5-cm.) margins and a 1-inch (2½-cm.) border, so your blocks turn out to be 4 inches (10 cm.) square, and, therefore, 56 × 56 stitches.

In analyzing the design blocks in this book you will find that most of them turn out to be between 56 × 56 stitches and 64 × 64 stitches. You will discover, if you are doing an average-sized pillow, that this is the range your blocks will fall into. Of course, there is no set rule. You might, for example, want a 12-inch (30½-cm.) square pillow with one large 8-inch (20-cm.) Pieced Star and a 2-inch (5-cm.) margin.

As you can see, the size of the finished piece very definitely controls the size of the block. Of course, if you do not care about the size of your finished piece, you can just go ahead and decide the size of your block first. As far as margins are concerned, it is usually a good idea to plan one, as it allows you to add on or take off a few extra spaces in your block or border where needed.

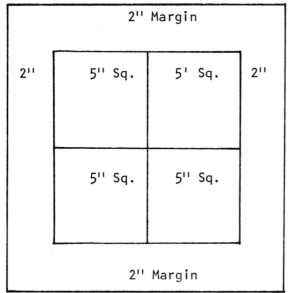

14'' Square

Figure 17

Simple line drawing of four blocks together with margin.

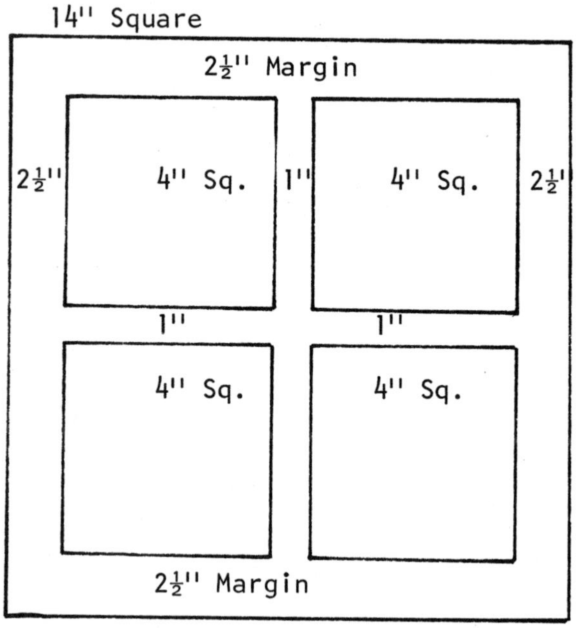

Figure 18

Simple line drawing of four blocks together with margin and 1-inch (2.5-cm.) spacing between blocks.

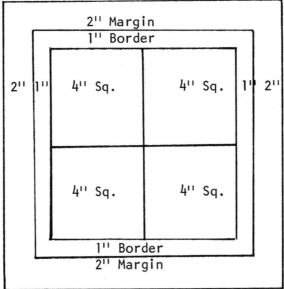

Figure 19

Simple line drawing of four blocks together with border and margin.

Remember, you are only doing this with a pencil to start, so play awhile. Of course, you could stitch an entire design with one single shape (see Mosaic Flowers, for example).

Planning the Block

Now you are ready to work out the design for your blocks. After having done the simple line drawing of your project, you see that your block turns out to be 56 × 56 stitches. Don't think about pattern or color yet. Now is the time to concentrate on planning shapes for your block, working them to fall within the borderline of the block. If your design does extend past the borderline a few spaces and you are using a margin, don't worry about it. If you are not using a margin, however, you must be exact. An advantage to using a margin, therefore, is that you can always make your block a little larger or smaller if necessary and still hold to the size of your finished piece. Sometimes, when drawing a block, I find that I like what is appearing on my paper, but that I'm so far out of my borderline I couldn't possibly keep to the original planned size. In cases like this, count the spaces that exceed the border and reduce the individual shapes to make the whole block fit. Also, remember that if your block shapes are too small, you will not be able to get much pattern within the blocks. For this reason I have included many small patterns in Part 4.

On the following pages you will find the various geometric figures, called "shapes," used to build block designs. These are the most common, and, once you have learned how to use them, you can go on and on with your own ideas. You might even invent new shapes. The shapes are easy to see separately, and together they form very beautiful designs. Look at the shapes on page 112 carefully. Taken from basic geometric figures, these shapes have been revised to accommodate the nature of counted cross-stitch. Each square of the graph represents a stitch and each row of the graph represents a row of stitches. The "steps," moving up or down, left or right, form the shape.

These shapes are named according to the geometric figure they most closely represent. For our purposes rhomboids are two triangles together. If you drew an imaginary line straight through the center of any of these rhomboids, you would have two triangles.

Before you actually begin to work out the shapes for your blocks, it's important that you understand something about color relationships and the role they play in design. Experiment with different shapes on graph paper and then decide which one you want to be predominant. Think in black, gray, and white. Three simple blocks are shown in Figures 20, 21, and 22. They all start with an angled square and each one consists of sixteen triangles. All three are exactly the same size and are made up of exactly the same shapes. In the three examples the darkest shapes are predominant, the speckled ones are secondary, and the white is background. You can see how the look of a design can be completely changed this way. When planning your colors, remember that dark colors project and that light colors recede. Study old patchwork quilts. You will notice that a good deal of contrast was used in order to bring out shapes.

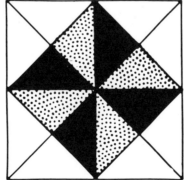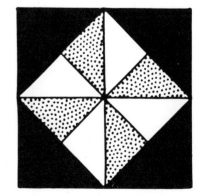

Figures 20, 21, and 22

Notice the visual difference between these three drawings. All three are the same, except for color. Three different looks are achieved, due to dark, medium, and light tones.

SHAPES

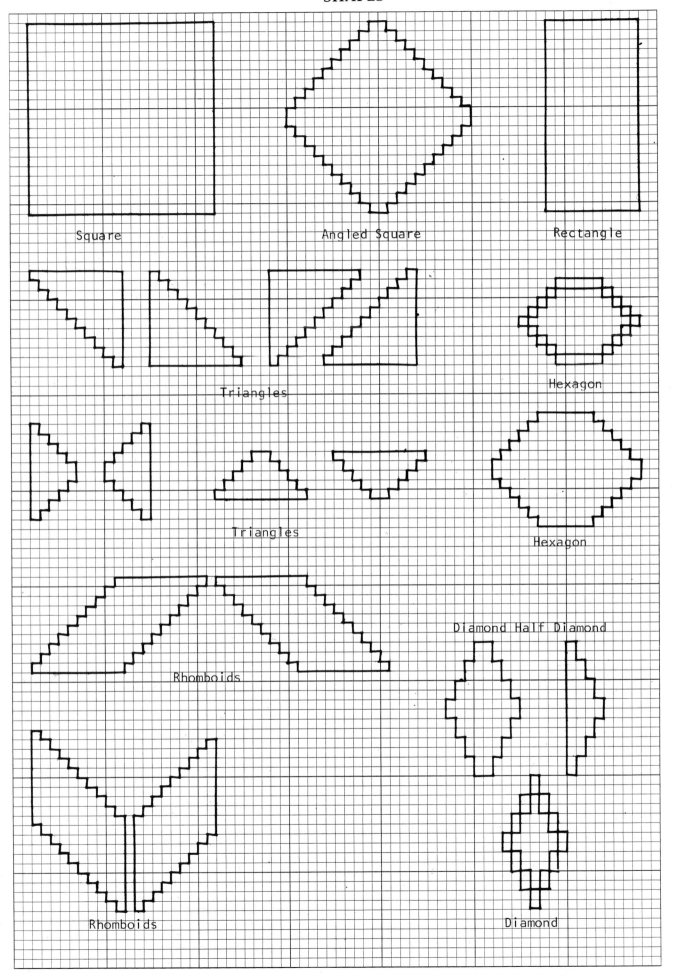

Square   Angled Square   Rectangle

Triangles   Hexagon

Triangles   Hexagon

Diamond Half Diamond

Rhomboids

Rhomboids   Diamond

See page 114. All of the blocks on this page are configurations of triangles around a square. They all originated with the basic triangle—A.

In B, eight triangles are used to form an eight-pointed star. The square is ten spaces horizontally and ten spaces vertically. The triangles are built by fives around the square. There are 20 × 20 spaces in total. If you wanted this block to be larger, you would add spaces by twos to the square. You could make it the square 12 × 12, for example, as was done in C. This affects the triangles, which should now be built by sixes and sevens. If you choose to make this block smaller, use the same principle and subtract by twos. Unless you use solid color, as I have done in some of the block designs, never make your shape too small or you will not be able to work pattern within it. Triangular shapes are predominant in Le Moyne Star, Pieced Star, Hovering Hawks, Double Pinwheel, Autumn Leaves, and Queen Charlotte's Crown. Winged Square and Tree of Life are very simple blocks based on triangles. Also, if you look at Tulips and Cactus Rose, you will see that they are both based on B, the eight-pointed star shape. D, E, and F are examples of things that can happen using triangles. Triangles are fun to work with, and are an easy geometric to design with. Perhaps that is why old quilt patterns use more triangle shapes than any other.

Refer to the angled squares and the rhomboid on page 115. Both these shapes can be incorporated together and singly to make interesting blocks. D and F are two blocks that use angled squares and rhomboids together. These blocks are taken from cube patterns.

F is a slight alteration of the block in D, yet it looks very different. The rhomboids are now three spaces by six rows, which completely changes the design, and, through the use of color, this block could even be made into a flower design. You could also add the leaf pattern from E, which is a very effective way to convey leaves.

An overall design could be made from D by adding more shapes.

Other good examples of blocks that incorporate rhomboids and/or angled squares are Cactus Rose, Jackson Star, Joseph's Coat of Many Colors, Ring Around the Star, and Star of Bethlehem. For examples of rhomboids as leaves see Cactus Rose and Tulips.

G is an overall design and could conceivably be a 4-inch (10-cm.) block or a 12-inch (30-cm.) block for a finished project, depending on how large you make your rhomboids. When using an overall design for a finished piece, it must be balanced—north to south, east to west—even if you end in the middle of a shape. The slash lines are to show you that if the block ended at those lines it would still look fine. The design must, however, be the same on both sides. Draw your overall design on graph paper first, taping two sheets together, if necessary, on the wrong side. Make sure you line up your graph lines to each other when taping.

There are two ways of handling the hexagon shape. A and B on page 116 are examples. A is six spaces across the first row × twelve rows, the two center rows having the same count. When using this shape there is a basic rule: No matter how many spaces you have across the first row, the rows are always doubled. Example: four spaces first row—eight rows; five spaces first row—ten rows. The two center rows must always have the same stitch count. This enables one hexagon to be attached to another in an overall design, without the need for outlining. C and E are put together in this way.

B is another type of hexagon shape. The difference here is this shape must be outlined in another color. With this shape one hexagon becomes a part of the next one. The other difference between the two types of hexagons is that there is only one center row in this second type. D consists of this type of hexagon group, and Flower Garden was stitched using this type of hexagon.

Be aware of how you color any overall pattern if you do not want to outline. For example, if you are using one shape with one pattern next to a different shape with another pattern, but both patterns use the color of the fabric as part of the pattern, you may have a problem seeing the individual shapes. They could appear to run into each other. The greens in Mosaic had to be outlined for this reason. The pinks did not have to be outlined, because even though they do run into each other, or seem to, they do not actually spoil the visual look.

See page 117. These shapes can be used as an overall design as in D or as a flower design as in G in much the same way that hexagon shapes are usually used.

TRIANGLES

ANGLED SQUARES AND RHOMBOIDS

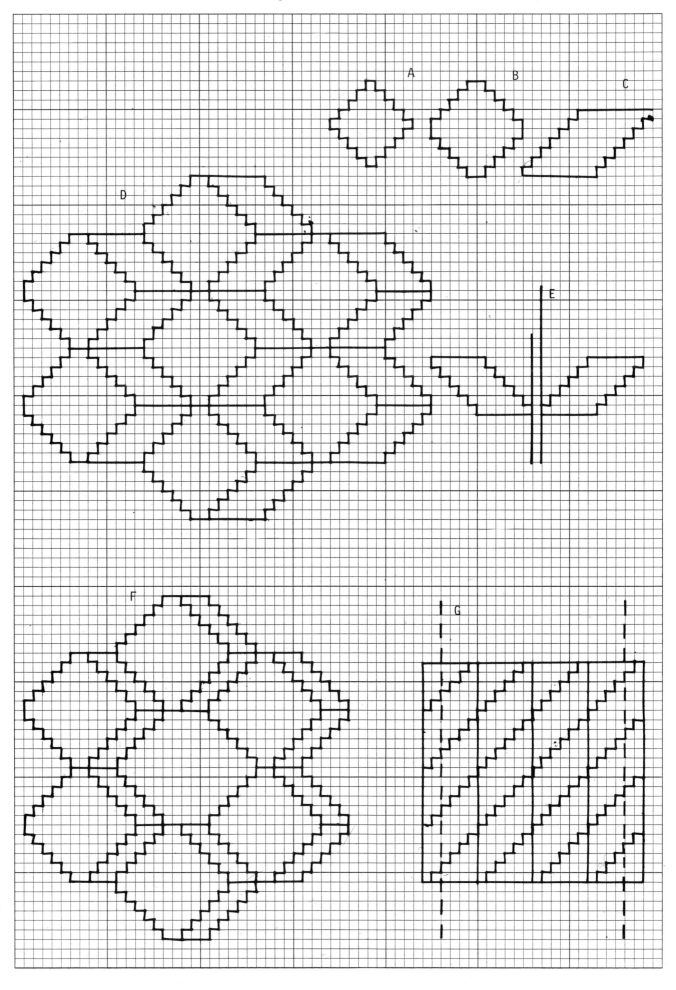

HEXAGONS

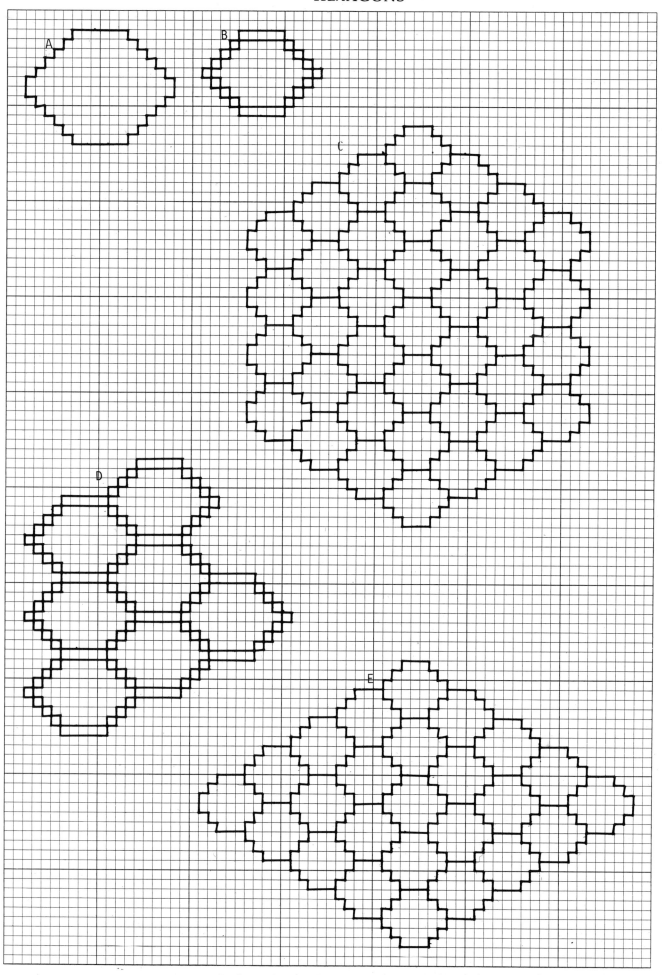

DIAMONDS

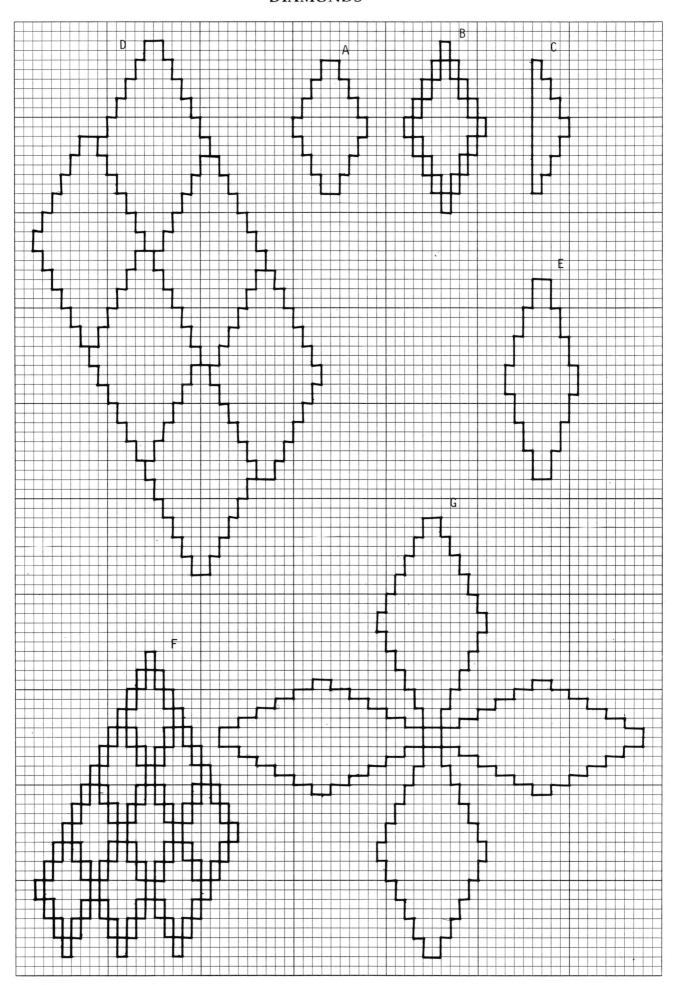

There are two types of diamonds just as there are two types of hexagons. In A there are two spaces across the first two rows, two spaces across the last two rows, and the two center rows are of the same count. Each step in the diamond drops down two rows. If you drop by three or more rows at a time, you would achieve an elongated diamond shape. (See E.)

B is the other diamond shape and it must be outlined, as one shape seems to become part of the next. (See E.) The concept of working in diamonds, in this case, is the same as hexagons.

Turn to Kaleidoscope and Star Flower in Part 2. Both are based on the basic diamond pattern. The difference is that Kaleidoscope is more elongated and Star Flower is wider and shorter. Study their patterns and you will see how the diamond shape changes. Note too how Kaleidoscope is split into half diamonds through its distribution of color.

Planning the Border

Borders can be fun to work out and are an interesting part of these designs, just as they are on patchwork quilts. If you search out some of the museum booklets I have listed in the bibliography, you can see many variations on borders pictured with museum quilts.

The following charts on pages 119, 120, and 121 are not meant for pattern, but for shape. They will show you some of the various kinds of borders you can use with block designs. Most of them are taken from old quilt borders. The symbols are given to show count, and the change of symbols within each border is to show you where to change color or pattern. You can enlarge or reduce each shape as you choose.

Corners are important and can get tricky. Make sure all four corners of any project are the same and that they are balanced. Sometimes you may have to reverse a border at the center of a project. (See Winged Square Project—A border.) You might try working from the right-hand corner toward the center, then the left-hand corner toward the center. If you do not meet evenly in the center, sometimes your pattern can be changed slightly in the center to make an interesting effect. To miter corners with pattern, do a few inches of pattern on graph paper, then hold a small square makeup mirror upright and diagonally over the pattern, and you will see how a mitered corner should look. Copy from what you see. Work the border out on graph paper and make sure the count is correct. Follow the guidelines of any of the projects in this book as reference for borders.

The border on the upper left, page 119, is a simple border and the border on the upper right is the same border with a pattern added. You can add pattern to any of these borders, using the pattern pages and the same concept as adding pattern for a block design.

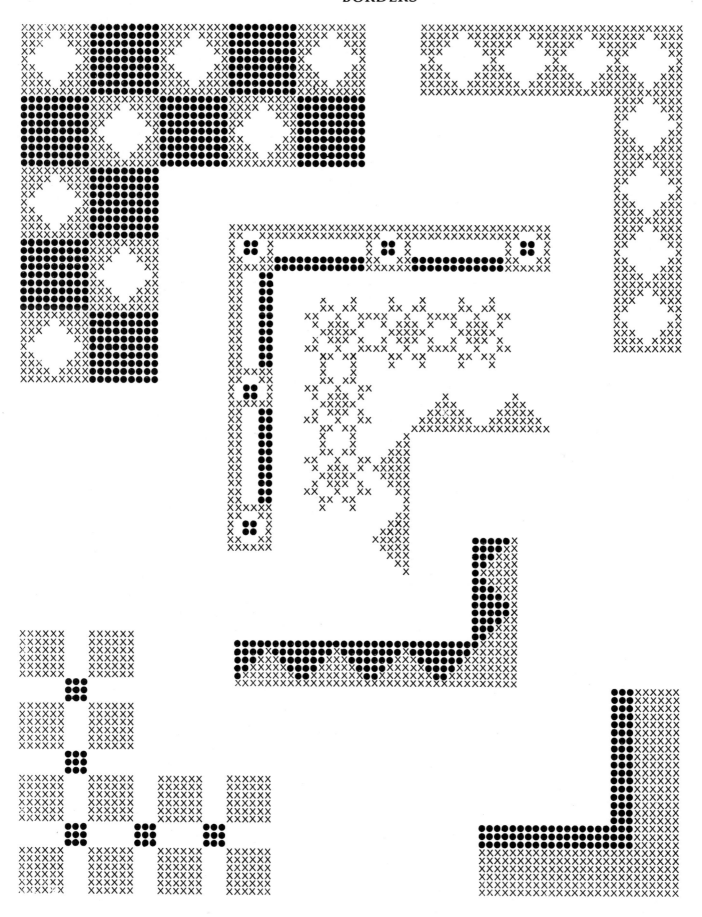

BIBLIOGRAPHY

Bordes, Marilynn Johnson. *Twelve Great Quilts from the American Wing*. New York: The Metropolitan Museum of Art, 1974.

Carlisle, Lilian Baker. *Pieced Work and Applique Quilts at Shelburne Museum*. Shelburne, Vt.: The Shelburne Museum, 1957.

Curtis, Phillip H. *American Quilts in the Newark Museum Collection*. Newark, New Jersey: The Newark Museum, 1973.

Eldredge, Charles C. and Museum Staff. *Quilters Choice*. Lawrence, Kansas: Helen Foresman Spencer Museum of Art, 1978.

Finley, Ruth E. *Old Patchwork Quilts and the Women Who Made Them*. 1929. Reprint, Newton Centre, Mass.: Charles T. Branford Co., 1970.

Gutcheon, Beth and Jeffrey. *The Quilt Design Workbook*. New York: Rawson Associates, 1976.

Hall, Carrie A., and Fretsinger, Rose. *The Romance of the Patchwork Quilt in America*. New York: Bonanza Books, Reprint, 1935.

Holstein, Jonathan. *The Pieced Quilt—An American Design Tradition*. New York: New York Graphic Society Ltd., 1973.

Ickes, Marguerite. *The Standard Book of Quiltmaking and Collecting*. New York: Dover Publications, 1959.

Katzenberg, Dena S. *The Great American Cover-Up; Counterpanes of the Eighteenth and Nineteenth Centuries*. Baltimore, Md.: The Baltimore Museum of Art, 1971.

McKim, Ruby. *One Hundred and One Patchwork Patterns*. New York: Dover Publications, 1962.

Orlofsky, Myron and Patsy. *Quilts in America*. New York: McGraw Hill, 1974.

Safford, Carleton, and Bishop, Robert. *America's Quilts and Coverlets*. New York: E. P. Dutton, 1972.

Schoenfeld, Susan. *Pattern Design for Needlepoint and Patchwork*. New York: Van Nostrand Reinhold Company, 1974.

INDEX

ACKNOWLEDGMENTS

To my daughter Patricia Lynch, who is responsible for stitching many of the block designs and finished pieces used in this book, thank you, Patty, for being there when I needed you.

A very special thanks to Jesse Blackman, not only for your expert needlework, but also for your companionship and support.

Thank you, Bonnie Flemming, for all your time and effort in stitching many of the block designs.

To my editor, Susan Rosenthal Gies, thank you for your valuable suggestions and comments, as well as your time and effort.

My thanks to Nancy Newman Green. Because of your support this book is being published.

To all of the other people too numerous to name, who had any part in the making of this book, my thanks.